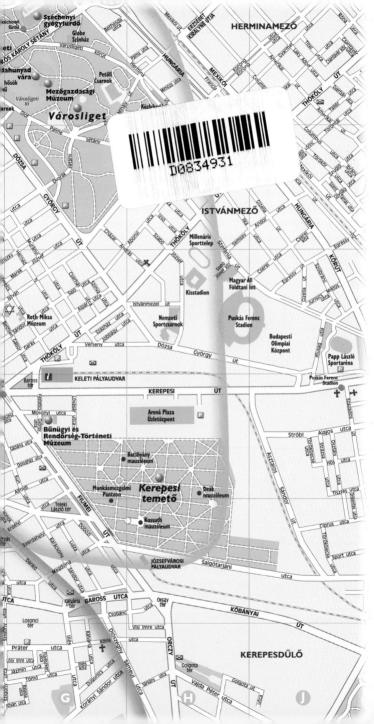

Fodor's
25 Best

BUDAPEST

How to Use This Book

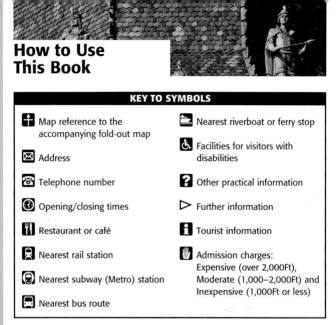

KEY TO SYMBOLS

✚ Map reference to the accompanying fold-out map

✉ Address

☎ Telephone number

🕐 Opening/closing times

🍴 Restaurant or café

🚊 Nearest rail station

Ⓜ Nearest subway (Metro) station

🚌 Nearest bus route

🚢 Nearest riverboat or ferry stop

♿ Facilities for visitors with disabilities

❓ Other practical information

▷ Further information

ℹ Tourist information

✋ Admission charges: Expensive (over 2,000Ft), Moderate (1,000–2,000Ft) and Inexpensive (1,000Ft or less)

This guide is divided into four sections

● Essential Budapest: An introduction to the city and tips on making the most of your stay.

● Budapest by Area: We've broken the city into six areas, and recommended the best sights, shops, entertainment venues, nightlife and places to eat in each one. Suggested walks help you to explore on foot.

● Where to Stay: The best hotels, whether you're looking for luxury, budget or something in between.

● Need to Know: The info you need to make your trip run smoothly, including getting about by public transport, weather tips, emergency phone numbers and useful websites.

Navigation In the Budapest by Area chapter, we've given each area its own color, which is also used on the locator maps throughout the book and the map on the inside front cover.

Maps The fold-out map accompanying this book is a comprehensive street plan of Budapest. The grid on this fold-out map is the same as the grid on the locator maps within the book. We've given grid references within the book for each sight and listing.

Contents

Introducing Budapest

Since shaking off the last shackles of communism in 1991, Budapest has quickly developed into one of Europe's most enticing capitals. Boasting an exciting and elegant range of sights and styles, it has something to appeal to all tastes.

For much of its history, Budapest's was a tale of two cities. The famous Chain Bridge—the first permanent structure here to span the Danube—wasn't opened until 1849, and before that the river formed a barrier separating the communities on each side. The characters of Buda (to the west of the river) and Pest (to the east) remain very different to this day. Buda holds the palace and medieval Castle District, before giving way to leafy hills. Pest is the financial and commercial heart, home to the Parliament building, the business district and the main concentration of shops, restaurants and bars.

What makes Budapest an enchanting spot for a city break is the variety it offers. On any given day you're likely to encounter art-nouveau mansions, a neo-Gothic church topped with vivid roof tiles and pastel medieval houses. You'll stroll along boulevards and quaint cobbled alleys, relax in lush parks or paved squares, browse bustling markets or shopping malls, have cake in a *fin-de-siècle* café or a beer in a lively bar. And there are plenty of museums and galleries covering interests to appeal to most visitors.

Even during the Communist period, Hungary always leaned toward the West. It's a cosmopolitan capital. Conference hotels and modern business areas have appeared, and a programme to spruce up the city's facades is ongoing. But despite this, an aura of history and hard times past is evident in the occasional bullet hole from 1956 and a flaking 19th-century town house. It's this tangible mix of the past and promise of tomorrow that makes Budapest so enchanting.

FACTS AND FIGURES

- Population: 1,774,000
- Size: 525sq km (203sq miles)
- Time: Central European Time (winter: GMT+1; summer: GMT+2)
- Telephone code: 0036 (country), 1 (city)
- Nickname: "Pearl of the Danube"
- Currency: Hungarian forint (Ft or HUF)

BUDAPEST'S FAMOUS

Albert Szent-Györgyi Discovered Vitamin C, which he extracted from paprika.
László Bíró Invented the ballpoint pen after tiring of ink spills.
Ferenc Liszt/Béla Bartók Two of the country's greatest composers.
Ernő Rubik Creator of the famous cube puzzle in the 1980s.

SPA CAPITAL

Landlocked it may be, but Hungary has water in abundance. The earth's crust is relatively thin in this region, and natural thermal water emerges through springs and drilled boreholes. There is a rich bathing tradition. The Romans soaked in Budapest almost 2,000 years ago, and the capital has around 50 baths—more than any other world capital.

NAVIGATION

Finding your way around Budapest is simple. The Danube splits Pest from Buda. The middle of Pest contains two semicircular ring roads crossed by straight boulevards radiating outward. The heart of Buda consists of the Castle and Gellért hills rising above the river. The city is divided among 23 districts. The middle digits in a postcode indicate the district—so an address with a postcode of H-1024 is in Buda's District II.

A Short Stay in Budapest

DAY 1

Morning Begin your day at 8.30 with a ride up Castle Hill aboard the **Sikló** (funicular, ▷ 32). Take an early-morning stroll around the streets of the Castle District before the crowds arrive. Drop in on **Mátyás templom** (▷ 30) before heading to Bécsi kapu tér and following the outer walls around the northern tip of the district for views over the **Buda Hills** (▷ 103).

Mid-morning Stop for a cake at **Ruszwurm** (▷ 36) and then walk to the castle complex at the southern end. There you'll find one of the country's leading collections of national art at the **Hungarian National Gallery** (▷ 28–29).

Lunch Several of the cafés and restaurants in the Castle District are overpriced. Instead try **Café Pierrot** (▷ 36) or **Baltazar** (▷ 36).

Afternoon Leave the Castle District and take a tram from Széll Kálmán tér to the lower station of the **Cogwheel Railway**. On alighting, either follow one of the trails on foot to **János-hegy** (▷ 103) or take the **Children's Railway** there. This hill offers pretty walking routes and a lookout tower. After that, ride the chairlift down the hillside and take bus No. 291 to Nyugati, on the Pest side of the river.

Dinner If you plan to go to the opera, consider **Két szerecsen** (▷ 62), **Callas** (▷ 61) or a restaurant-bar on Liszt Ferenc tér.

Evening Take in a performance at the wonderful **State Opera House** (▷ 52), relax over a few drinks on the bustling Liszt Ferenc tér, check out a fun and vibrant ruin pub (▷ 71) or dance at a club on Hajógyári-sziget.

Morning Start the day by visiting two of Pest's primary landmarks: the Westminster-inspired neo-Gothic **Parliament** building (▷ 54–55) on Kossuth tér and the looming **Szent István Bazilika** (▷ 56–57), home to Hungary's most holy relic.

Mid-morning After that, stroll along the pedestrianized **Váci utca** (▷ 72), the city's main shopping street. Finish off by browsing the lace and food at the many stalls of the **Great Market Hall** (▷ 75).

Lunch Stay with the lively market atmosphere for good value dishes at **Fakanál** (▷ 81). Alternatively, a good place to stop for a central, filling and well-priced lunch is **Fatál** (▷ 81), just off Váci utca.

Afternoon Take a look around the massive **Hungarian National Museum** (▷ 68) before following the Small Boulevard northward to the start of **Andrássy út** (▷ 86). You can choose either to walk the whole of its 2km (1 mile) or take the underground that runs below. The avenue culminates at **Heroes' Square** (▷ 87), containing the **Museum of Fine Arts** (▷ 88–89). Beyond is the lush **City Park** (▷ 91), where you shouldn't miss the quirky-looking **Vajdahunyad Castle** (▷ 94). Finish things off with a relaxing soak in the neo-baroque **Széchenyi Baths** (▷ 93).

Dinner If you fancy splashing out, enjoy an elegant dinner at **Gundel** (▷ 98, reserve ahead). Otherwise eat at **Bagolyvár** (▷ 98), its less expensive sister restaurant next door.

Evening Stroll the Pest riverside to enjoy the bridge illuminations, before choosing from the many lively café-bars on Ráday utca.

Top 25

TOP
25

ESSENTIAL BUDAPEST TOP 25

▶ ▶ ▶

Andrássy út ▷ 86–87
Elegant boulevard built
to emulate the Champs-
Élysées in Paris.

Városliget ▷ 91 The
capital's primary park with
a zoo, circus, boating lake
and castle.

Váci utca ▷ 72 Bustling
street of shops and cafés
at the heart of the city; this
is the tourists' preferred
shopping area.

Terror Háza Múzeum
▷ 90 Museum dedicated
to the victims of Hungary's
Nazi and Communist
terror regimes.

Memento Park
▷ 104 Resting place for
Communist statues
erected during Soviet rule.

Szépművészeti Múzeum
▷ 88–89 A breathtaking
collection of international
fine art including Old
Masters.

Szent István Bazilika
▷ 56–57 Basilica that
contains the mummified
hand of Hungary's first
Christian king.

Aquincum ▷ 102 A rich
cluster of archaeological
remains from the Roman
period.

Budai-hegység ▷ 103
Buda's leafy hills—a
pretty backdrop for walks
and bike rides.

Romkocsma ▷ 71 Ruin
pubs have thrift-shop decor
and a quirky vibe that's
unique to Budapest.

Országház ▷ 54–55
Majestic Parliament
building modelled on that
in London.

Néprajzi Múzeum ▷ 53
Display of traditional
costumes and other
national folk items.

8

These pages are a quick guide to the Top 25, which are described in more detail later. Here they are listed alphabetically, and the tinted background shows which area they are in.

Budapesti Történeti Múzeum ▷ 24 Collection of historical artefacts in Buda Castle Palace.

Budavári Palota ▷ 26–27 Former royal palace overlooking the Danube from Castle Hill.

Danube Boat Trip ▷ 66 Take a romantic river ride on the Danube by night or by day.

Gellért-hegy ▷ 40 Rugged hill capped with the stocky citadel.

Halászbástya ▷ 25 Turreted monument named after the fishermen who once defended this part of Castle Hill.

Hotel Gellért and Gellért gyógyfürdő ▷ 41 Budapest's best-known historic hotel and popular thermal baths.

Iparművészeti Múzeum ▷ 67 Exhibition of arts and crafts in a stunning art-nouveau building.

Magyar Állami Operaház ▷ 52 Extravagant state opera house.

Magyar Nemzeti Galéria ▷ 28–29 Huge collection of Hungarian art dating from the medieval period.

Magyar Nemzeti Múzeum ▷ 68–69 This museum is the country's biggest.

Margit-sziget ▷ 42–43 Leafy island lying in the Danube between Margit and Árpád bridges.

Nagy Zsinagóga and Zsidó Múzeum ▷ 70 World's second-largest synagogue, with a museum.

Mátyás templom ▷ 30 Striking Mátyás Church was built during the 1896 millenary celebrations.

SPORTÁRDÚLŐ

Szépművészeti Múzeum

HERMINAMEZŐ

Városliget

Andrássy út

ISTVÁNMEZŐ

Reiner F park

RZSÉBÉTVAROS

Kerepesi temető

OKTOGON TO VÁROSLIGET 83-98

JÓZSEFVAROS

KEREPESDŰLŐ

Iparművészeti Múzeum

Orczy kert

AROUND BELVÁROS 63-82

Népliget

Shopping

Budapest is a modern capital, and there is no shortage of designer boutiques selling expensive fashion accessories, and slick shopping malls hosting many stores over several floors. However, traditional goods are very much to the fore in quaint craftshops, and you'll find interesting and well-priced food in a range of markets. Antiques aren't difficult to find and a glut of bookshops is evidence of the Hungarian cerebral side.

Food

Hungarians are immensely proud of their cuisine. The places to head to buy fresh, tasty produce are the indoor and outdoor markets. The most atmospheric are the market halls (*vásárcsarnok*); several of these date back to the 19th century, the most famous being the Great (or Central) Market Hall (Nagycsarnok) facing the southern end of Váci utca. Food specialties include sausages and salamis, paprika (a red pepper that is added to many native dishes and is available either whole or ground) and goose liver.

Antiques

The prime area for antiques hunters is Falk Miksa utca in Pest, near Margaret Bridge. This street is lined with antiques shops and galleries selling everything from clocks to fine furniture. Some of the more popular tourist spots (like Váci utca and the Castle District) have stores selling antiques too, but be wary of high prices.

BUY THE BOTTLE

Hungary has 22 wine regions and since the fall of Communism the quality has improved steadily with private investment. Look out for bottles of Tokaji Aszú, a white and usually sweet wine, often with honeyed yet fresh notes, which is very well regarded among connoisseurs. Louis XIV famously referred to it as the "King of Wines, Wine of Kings." Alternatively, go for a fruit brandy (*pálinka*) or Unicum, a bitter-tasting herbal liqueur.

Window-shopping; salamis and sausages; Váci utca (top to bottom)

Elsewhere, you'll find several shops or auction houses operated by a company called BÁV. Be sure to check you are issued with any necessary export permit when buying. There are antiquarian bookshops selling old books, maps and prints opposite the Hungarian National Museum (on Múzeum körút).

Porcelain, Arts and Crafts

The town of Herend, to the north of Lake Balaton, is famous for its fine porcelain—both practical tableware and decorative figurines—and pieces are readily available in antiques stores and dedicated outlets. The other big name in the world of Hungarian ceramics is Zsolnay. The factory, which was established in 1853 in Pécs, produces bold and distinctive pieces—indeed, it is responsible for the brightly colored roof tiles adorning some of the city's landmark buildings, including the Mátyás Church. Folk centers and the Great Market Hall offer arts and crafts, comprising pottery, lace and wooden toys.

Clothes and Shopping Malls

You'll find boutiques selling labels that are beyond the reach of most Hungarians in the heart of Pest, and particularly along the tourist-heavy Váci utca. Considerably cheaper clothes shops hug the two Pest ringroads (Kiskörút and Nagykörút). Major brands and fashion retailers are found in the big shopping malls, the main central ones being Mammut, Mom Park and Westend City Center.

A CHRISTMAS CRACKER

If you're there at the right time, it's worth browsing the Christmas Market (running throughout December) in Vörösmarty tér. The square—with its statue of poet Mihály Vörösmarty cocooned in plastic to prevent the marble from cracking in the cold—is filled with dozens of stalls displaying handcrafted items that make excellent gifts. Make sure to refuel with a doughnut tower (kürtőskalács) and a cup of spiced wine!

Shopping by Theme

Whether you're looking for a department store or a quirky boutique, or something in between, you'll find it all in Budapest. On this page shops are listed by theme. For a more detailed write-up, see the individual listings in Budapest by Area.

Art and Antiques
Várfok galéria (▷ 34)

Books and Music
Alexandra Books (▷ 59)
Libri Studium (▷ 78)
Litea (▷ 34)

China and Glass
Ajka kristály (▷ 59, 77)
Herendi porcelán (▷ 77)
Zsolnay porcelán (▷ 78)

Fashion
Attila Shoes (▷ 77)
Eclectick Design (▷ 77)
Hugo Boss (▷ 77)
Jackpot and Cottonfield
   (▷ 77)
Tisza cipő (▷ 78)

Food and Drink
Borszakúzlet (▷ 77)
Bortársaság (▷ 34)
Fény Utcai Piac (▷ 34)
Prés Ház Wine Shop and
   Museum (▷ 78)
Szamos Marcipán
   (▷ 78)

Gifts
Dísz téri piac (▷ 34)
Folkart Kézművesház
   (▷ 77)
Maciművek (▷ 59)

Markets
Christmas Market (▷ 77)
Fény utcai piac (▷ 34)
Lehel Market (▷ 59)
Vásárcsarnok (▷ 75, 78)

Shopping Areas
Andrássy út (▷ 59)
Falk Miksa utca (▷ 59)
Király utca (▷ 77)
Mammut (▷ 34)
Szent István tér (▷ 59)
Párisi Nagyáruház
   (▷ 59)

Budapest by Night

Budapest is brilliant by night, with its buildings well lit and its squares busy. Those seeking culture can enjoy performances of music and dance at any time of the year (from opera to jazz), while there are plenty of bars and clubs for the party-goers. During the warmer months everyone moves outside to courtyard bars and riverside beach-style clubs, and there are regular alfresco concerts.

Hot Spots
Pest has the greater number of bars and restaurants. Liszt Ferenc tér—straddling Andrássy út—has traditionally proved a preferred early-evening meeting place. Surrounded with modern café-bars, it fills with people sitting at tables in summer. In recent years, however, an alternative strip has emerged on Ráday utca, right in the heart of the city. This, too, is lined with a good choice of bars and some feel the service is better and the clientele more down-to-earth. Cafés and bars along the river are frequently attached to hotels and are consequently expensive. Shipyard Island hosts several lively nightclubs, which are outdoor venues in summer.

Evening Stroll
The promenades running either side of the Danube are perfect for a romantic walk. Several of the bridges are illuminated—the Chain Bridge looks truly stunning—and, with Buda Castle Palace and Parliament casting reflections in the dark water, the views are magical.

HOT IN THE CITY

In summer, temporary bars and clubs spring up, often occupying disused courtyards or gardens, and moving location from year to year. As such, they can be difficult to find and only become popular through word of mouth. Szimplakert (in the Jewish District) started as a pop-up and has gone on to be a year-round favorite, giving rise to a series of now-famous ruin pubs (▷ 71).

The illuminated Parliament building at night; Tokaji wine; a popular bar; a candlelit dinner (top to bottom)

Where to Eat

Hungary's position in Central Europe and its history of occupation by foreign powers means that its cuisine draws on many influences, including German, Austrian, Turkish and Serb. Today there is a wide variety of restaurants to please any taste and wallet.

What to Expect
Home to one of Central Europe's most vibrant food scenes, Budapest can offer an eclectic choice that ranges from fine-dining restaurants to neighborhood cafés, traditional Hungarian fare to fusion and world cuisine—all served up in settings from old-world grandeur and coffee-house charm to the off-beat decor of ruin pubs. Restaurants in Budapest are usually open between midday and around 11pm, but it's safest to arrive before 10pm. With the exception of very exclusive restaurants, there is no formal dress code.

The Choice
The most common word for restaurant is *étterem*, although you might also come across *vendéglő* and *csárda,* the latter specializing in traditional food. As well as Hungarian, many world cuisines are represented. Chinese buffet-style eateries are popular for quick and inexpensive meals; it's also worth looking out for two- or three-course set tourist menus offered between certain hours of the day. Coffee and cake are ubiquitous in Budapest, and there are some grand cafés. Pâtisseries (*cukrászda*) sell cakes to take away.

TIPPING

It's acceptable to tip 10 percent in restaurants or to round up a café bill, but always check that service is not included. If you wish to tip, do not leave cash on the table. Instead, indicate the total you wish to pay when the bill is brought to you. If you say "thank you" as you hand over your money, the staff will assume that you don't require any change and keep the difference as a tip.

Budapest has many restaurants and cafés where you can eat and drink alfresco

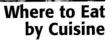

Where to Eat by Cuisine

There are plenty of places to eat to suit all tastes and budgets in Budapest. On this page they are listed by cuisine. For a more detailed description of each restaurant, see Budapest by Area.

Budapest's Best
Búsuló Juhász (▷ 48)
Callas (▷ 61)
Costes (▷ 81)
Gundel (▷ 98)
Halászbástya (▷ 36)
Klassz (▷ 98)
Mak Bisztro (▷ 62)
Onyx (▷ 82)
Spoon–the Boat (▷ 82)

Coffeehouses
Café Pierrot (▷ 36)
Central kávéház (▷ 80)
Európa kávéház (▷ 62)
Gerbeaud (▷ 81)
Múzeum (▷ 82)
Nagyi palacsintázója
   (▷ 82)
New York kávéház
   (▷ 82)
Ruszwurm (▷ 36)

Hungarian
Arany Bárány (▷ 80)
Arany Kaviár (▷ 36)
Bagolyvár (▷ 98)
Baltazár (▷ 36)
Café Kör (▷ 61)
Fakanál (▷ 81)
Fatál (▷ 81)
Kárpátia (▷ 81)
Kispiac Bisztro (▷ 62)
La Perle Noire (▷ 98)
Margitkert (▷ 48)
Mátyás pince (▷ 81)
Pesti Diszno (▷ 62)
Speiz (▷ 36)
Trófea Grill (▷ 48)

International
Indigo (▷ 98)
Két szerecsen (▷ 62)
Kollázs Brasserie (▷ 62)
Robinson (▷ 98)
Spinoza Café (▷ 82)

Italian
Két Szerecsen (▷ 62)
Magdalena Merlo (▷ 98)
Trattoria Toscana (▷ 82)

Top Tips For...

These great suggestions will help you tailor your ideal visit to Budapest, no matter how you choose to spend your time. Each suggestion has a fuller write-up elsewhere in the book.

CLIMBING HIGH

Ride the funicular (▷ 32) to the Castle District, overlooking the river from the Buda bank.
Take a leg-sapping walk up Gellért Hill (▷ 40) to visit the Citadella (▷ 45) and get a close-up of the Freedom Monument (▷ 44 and 46).
Climb up Szent István Bazilika (▷ 56) to the gallery running around the outside of its dome and fabulous city views.

ENTERTAINING THE KIDS

Take them up to the hills on the Children's Railway (▷ 103).
Spend an afternoon at Városliget (▷ 91), to row or skate on the lake, and visit the circus.
Hit the zoo (▷ 92) and get a close look at its 2,000 species. Take time yourself to admire the art-nouveau elephant house.
Get interactive at the family-friendly Natural History Museum (▷ 74).
Go pedaling by hiring a buggy on Margit-sziget (▷ 42).

Riding the funicular (top); the Freedom Monument (above)

TAKING THE WATERS

Soak away your aches in one of the city's many thermal spas, such as Király gyógyfürdő (▷ 45) or Széchenyi gyógyfürdő (▷ 93).
Stroll along the banks of the River Danube on the Danube Promenade (▷ 73).
Take a trip to Lake Balaton (▷ 105), the largest lake in Central Europe.
Reserve seats on a romantic river cruise along the Danube (▷ 66), by day or by night.

Cruise along the River Danube (above right); a game of chess in a thermal spa (right)

Váci utca; taking a walk in one of the city's green spaces (below)

WHAT'S FREE

Visit St. Stephen's Basilica (▷ 56–57).
Make the connection with a walk across the Chain Bridge (▷ 4), the first bridge to link Buda with Pest, and drink in the fantastic view.
Do some window shopping along Váci utca (▷ 72) and soak up the atmosphere in the bustling Nagycsarnok (▷ 75).

NATURE AND GREEN SPACES

Ride the Cogwheel Railway into the Buda Hills (▷ 103), climb the Erzsébet-kilátó (viewing tower) on János-hegy and take the chairlift down the side of the forested hill.
Enjoy the sun with a lazy hour in one of Budapest's leafy parks—Városliget (▷ 91) or Margit-sziget (▷ 42).

HUNGARIAN SPECIALTIES

Browse a market hall for some typical Hungarian produce and a bottle of Bull's Blood (▷ panel, 59) or Tokaji Aszú (▷ panel, 10).
Splash out on a meal at Gundel (▷ 98), a restaurant with a long tradition.
Go winetasting at Bortársaság (▷ 34).

Meat shop in a market hall (above); a streetside café (below)

CAFÉ SOCIETY

Find a table at the tiny Ruszwurm (▷ 36), the city's oldest café.
Order a portion of layered cake at the famous Gerbeaud café (▷ 81), named after the Swiss cake maker who managed it in the 1880s.
Sip a coffee and linger over a delicious cake at Európa kávéház (▷ 62).

ACCOMMODATION ON A SHOESTRING

Staying in Budapest doesn't have to break the bank

Reserve a private room or apartment through companies like Ibusz or Best Hotel Service (▷ panel, 109).

Stay in a prime minister's villa at Kalmár Pension (▷ 109), an antiques-filled place that was originally built for early-20th-century leader Pál Teleki.

Cater for yourself by choosing an apartment hotel like Adina (▷ 109), which have little kitchens so you can save on eating out.

DISCOVERING ART

Explore the monuments and dark secrets of the country's communist past in Memento Park (▷ 104) and House of Terror Museum (▷ 90).

Get a taste for Magyar art over the centuries in the Hungarian National Gallery (▷ 28).

Trawl the rich collection of the Hungarian National Museum (▷ 68) and the Roman objects at the Aquincum Museum (▷ 102).

THE ULTIMATE SOUVENIR

Pick up some traditional craftwork in one of several central shops such as Folkart Kézműveshaz on Váci utca (▷ 77).

Buy a piece of fine porcelain from a specialist company outlet like that representing Herend (▷ panel, 77) on József nádor tér.

Taste and purchase Hungarian wine from Bortársaság (▷ 34), the Wine Society with several shops in the city (including that on Batthyány utca).

Memento Park; mosaics at Aquincum (above)

A GREAT NIGHT OUT

Listen to live music at the prison-themed Alcatraz (▷ 79).

Head to Liszt Ferenc tér for a cocktail at Incognito (▷ 97) a long-standing favourite in the city.

Traditional Hungarian products for sale at a market stall (right)

Budapest by Area

Looking down over the river, the Castle District was once the fortified capital of the country and home to the royal court. It has changed its face over the centuries, having endured many savage sieges. Today, however, it holds several museums.

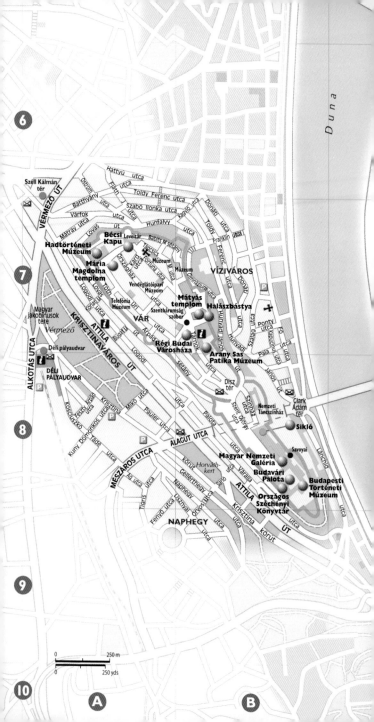

6

Duna

Széll Kálmán
tér

VÉRMEZŐ UT

Hattyú utca

Fürj utca

Toldy Ferenc utca

Batthyány utca

Szabó Ilonka utca

Várfok utca

Várfok utca

Donáti utca

Hunfalvy utca

Mátray utca

Lovas út

Bécsi
Kapu

Levéltár

Toldy Ferenc utca

Hadtörténeti
Múzeum

Mária
Magdolna
templom

Ostrom utca

Táncsics utca

Franklin utca

Babits M sétány

Múzeum

VÍZIVÁROS

Úri utca

Országház utca

Fortuna utca

Gimnázium utca

Múzeum

P

7

Magyar
jakobinusok
tere

Vérmező

Telefónia
Múzeum

Vendéglátóipari
Múzeum

Mátyás
templom

Halászbástya

KRISZTINAVÁROS

ATTILA UT

Lovas út

Logodi utca

Úri utca

VÁR

Szentháromság
szobor

Szentháromság tér

Hunyadi János út

Ponty utca

Fő utca

Iskola utca

Déli pályaudvar

Régi Budai
Városháza

Árpád utca

Tárnok utca

Dísz tér

Arany Sas
Patika Múzeum

Pala utca

Halász utca

Jégverem utca

DÉLI
PÁLYAUDVAR

ALKOTAS UTCA

P

Krisztina körút

Mikó utca

Pauler utca

Palota utca

Dísz
tér

SzentGyörgy utca

Színház utca

Úri utca

Nemzeti
Táncszínház

Clark
Ádám
tér

Lánchíd

8

Kővágó-Kossziko tér

Kuny Domokos utca

Győző utca

Fiáth János utca

MÉSZÁROS UTCA

Krisztina utca

ALAGÚT UTCA

Horváth-
kert

Vár-alja

Palota út

Lánchíd utca

János utca

Sikló

Savoyai

Magyar Nemzeti
Galéria

Budavári
Palota

Tigris utca

Fenyő utca

Gellérthegy utca

Naphegy utca

Ússány utca

ATTILA UT

Krisztina körút

Országos
Széchényi
Könyvtár

Budapesti
Történeti
Múzeum

NAPHEGY

Krisztina körút

9

0   250 m

0   250 yds

10

A

B

Budapesti Történeti Múzeum

Museum exterior (left); a 14th-century statue of a courtier in the Knights' Hall (right)

The Budapest History Museum offers a rare glimpse of the medieval palace lying deep beneath the current complex. These remains were uncovered during renovations and excavations following the savage bombardment of the Castle District at the end of World War II.

History of the city The floors above ground are dedicated to exhibits charting the city's history from the prehistoric age up to the present. There are finds left by the various tribes who ruled the region in the centuries before the arrival of the Magyars—ancestors of today's Hungarians—and a good chronological portrayal of the birth and growth of modern Budapest. The latter takes 1686 as its starting point, the year that Buda was extracted from Turkish rule by the Habsburgs, moves through the Great Flood of 1838 and the millennial celebrations of 1896, and culminates in the decades following the end of communism.

Down below Accessed via a basement below the museum are the scant remains of what was the medieval palace. The palace reached its zenith during the 15th-century rule of King Mátyás, whose court was one of Europe's Renaissance powerhouses. The Renaissance Hall contains objects dating from that period. The 14th-century statues of contemporary courtiers displayed in the Knights' Hall are valuable because few statues of this kind survived the Ottoman occupation.

The Fishermen's Bastion (left); statue of King István (right)

TOP 25

Halászbástya

Despite its medieval styling, the Fishermen's Bastion—so called because this was supposedly the area of the Castle District defended by members of the Guild of Fishermen—is actually little more than a century old.

Fishermen's Bastion The Fishermen's Bastion is the work of Frigyes Schulek, who added it in 1902 to complement the adjacent Mátyás Church (which he also designed). Unlike the painstakingly researched statue in front of it (▷ below), the formidable-looking neo-Romanesque structure is a work of pure fantasy and bears little relation to genuine medieval fortifications. The turrets represent the seven Magyar tribes that settled in Hungary at the end of the first millennium. These were nomadic people, reflected in the tent-like appearance of the bastion's turrets. The bastion's upper and lower levels afford good views over Pest (and in particular the Parliament building) across the river.

St. István statue Schulek's fanciful flight continues on the plinth of the bronze equestrian statue of King István, which stands in front of the bastion. King István was responsible for suppressing the country's pagan factions and introducing Christianity. On a relief at the rear of the plinth, the bearded architect imagines himself presenting the church to István. The statue was by Alajos Stróbl, who took a decade researching 11th-century riding garb and armor in his quest for medieval authenticity.

THE BASICS

fishermansbastion.com
✚ B7
✉ I, Szentháromság tér
🚌 16, 16A, 116
♿ Lower terrace good, upper terrace none
🎫 Lower terrace free, open 24 hours year round; upper terrace mid-Feb to mid-March, free, otherwise inexpensive

HIGHLIGHTS

● The fierce-looking, helmeted statues depicting the Magyar tribal leaders
● Views over the river
● The Chapel inside the Bastion

TIP

● Don't bother paying to reach the upper terrace—the views are very nearly as good from the lower level, and equally good from the area in front of Buda Castle Palace (which is free to enter).

CASTLE DISTRICT TOP 25

25

Budavári Palota

HIGHLIGHTS

● The bronze *turul*—a mythical bird said to have fathered Árpád's own father, and thus an ancestor of the Magyars—at the first entrance to the palace complex
● The Mátyás Well in a courtyard at the back of the palace

TIPS

● Head to the terrace at the front of the palace for some exquisite views of the city.
● You can take a lift up to the complex from Dózsa György tér.

Buda Castle Palace looms high over the river and is one of the city's enduring symbols. The once royal residence houses two of Budapest's main museums.

The early days Castle Hill first became a royal complex under Béla IV in the 13th century. Returning from exile to a country decimated by the Mongol invasion of 1241–42, he recognized the hill's defensive advantages and constructed a town on top with a castle and fortified walls. Later monarchs built their palaces at the southern end of the hill, the most impressive being that of King Mátyás Corvinus.

Renaissance king Mátyás was one of Europe's great 15th-century kings; his court was a hub of Renaissance culture. There are a few remains of

Buda Castle Palace, on the riverside, now contains the Hungarian National Gallery and the Budapest History Museum

his palace (as well as that of the earlier Gothic palace of King Zsigmond) in the Budapest History Museum.

More recent history The building was destroyed during the battle to eject the Turks in 1686, after which the Habsburgs constructed a palace in its place. Expansion after the Austro-Hungarian Compromise of 1867, under the renowned architects Miklós Ybl and Alajos Hauszmann, included lengthening the facade and adding a dome. During World War II, the Russians besieged the hill where the German army had retreated. Fighting was fierce and the palace was severely damaged once more. The reconstruction was heavily tailored to 20th-century tastes. The simple, neoclassical version of the dome is typical of this shift.

THE BASICS

budacastlebudapest.com

➕ B8

✉ I, Szent György tér 2

☎ 1 458 3000

🕐 Castle courtyards open access; National Gallery Tue–Sun 10–6; Budapest History Museum Mar–Oct Tue–Sun 10–6, Nov–Feb 10–4

🚌 5, 16, 16A, 116; tram: 56; Sikló (funicular railway)

♿ Mainly good (lift access to most—though not all—areas of museums and library)

Magyar Nemzeti Galéria

HIGHLIGHTS

● *The Visitation* (1506) by the anonymous Master MS (first floor, Wing D)
● *Thunderstorm over the Puszta* (1853) by Károly Lotz (first floor, Wing C)
● *Condemned Cell I* (1870) by Mihály Munkácsy (first floor, Wing B)
● *Pilgrimage to the Cedars of Lebanon* (1907) by Tivadar Csontváry Kosztka (second floor, Wing C)

TIP

● Book in advance for a guided tour—given the museum's size, it's well worth it to ensure you see only the best pieces

Spreading across four wings of the Buda Castle Palace, the Hungarian National Gallery holds 100,000 works and is the country's biggest and best collection of Hungarian art.

Early art The gallery started up during the 19th-century reform movement, epitomized by the irrepressibly energetic Count István Széchenyi, and displays works dating from the 10th century up to the modern era. It opens on the ground floor of Wing D with the Medieval and Renaissance Lapidarium, showcasing some church art and architectural pieces including painted panels and Gothic altarpieces from the 15th century. Also here are carved details from the palace of King Mátyás. Directly above on the first floor is a display of beautiful late-Gothic

Visitors looking at a portrait; a statue from the Middle Ages; a baroque painting; Hungarian coronation regalia, including a jewelled crown; Hungarian royal seals (clockwise from left)

winged altars and some late-Renaissance and baroque works (many of them once owned by the Eszterházy family).

19th- and 20th-century art Art from the 19th century occupies the rest of the first floor in Wings B and C. Keep an eye out for great names of the period like Károly Lotz, famous for his moody Romanticist landscape depictions of life on the *puszta*, and Mihály Munkácsy, whose late 19th-century works were often infused with powerful and somber social messages. The next floor is devoted to 20th-century artists. You won't miss the huge canvases by Tivadar Csontváry Kosztka and other highlights include portraits by József Rippl-Rónai, plein-air pieces by József Egry and expressionist works by Vilmos Aba-Novák.

THE BASICS

mng.hu
➕ B8
✉ I, Szent György tér 2
☎ 1 469 7180
🕐 Tue–Sun 10–6
🍴 Café
🚌 5, 16, 16A, 78, 116; tram: 56; Sikló (funicular)
♿ Good (access via wings A and B)
💵 Moderate; access to the dome: inexpensive
❓ Guided tour available

CASTLE DISTRICT TOP 25

Mátyás templom

Beautiful roof tiles adorn Mátyás Church (left and right)

THE BASICS

matyas-templom.hu
+ B7
✉ I, Szentháromság tér 2
☎ 1 489 0716
🕐 Mon–Fri 9–5, Sat 9–12, Sun 1–5
🚌 16, 16A, 116
♿ Mainly good (access via visitors' exit)
💷 Moderate
❓ Audio guide available in numerous languages

HIGHLIGHTS

● The 14th-century Maria portal, at the southern side of the church. The relief above it shows the assumption of the Virgin Mary
● Copies of the Hungarian Holy Crown up some stairs in the royal oratory

Located in the heart of the Castle District, its spire a prominent feature of the Buda riverscape, Mátyás Church is awash with color—from its roof tiles to the painted stone walls inside.

The background Mátyás Church—officially called the Church of Our Lady—was first constructed between 1255 and 1269 for Buda's German population, and a few scraps of masonry and stone carvings remain in the current incarnation. It underwent several reconstructions over the centuries and was used as a mosque by the Turks and for the coronation of Ferenc József in 1867. The main overhaul was commissioned at the close of the 19th century to celebrate the 1,000-year anniversary of the Magyar arrival. The architect Frigyes Schulek undertook meticulous research in his quest to revive the Gothic spirit of the original. Later it was used as a kitchen by German soldiers during World War II, then as a Soviet stable, before being restored in 1970.

Inside the church The interior is painted with patterns based on patches of surviving decoration from the Middle Ages. The frescoes showing famous moments in Hungary's history are by historicist artists Károly Lotz and Bertalan Székely. The Béla Chapel on the north side of the church contains the remains of the 12th-century King Béla III, while the St. László Chapel has a replica of the gold bust of László (the real one is held in Győr Cathedral).

ARANY SAS PATIKA MÚZEUM

Although a relatively small attraction, Golden Eagle Pharmacy Museum contains furnishings and interesting medical items from Buda's first pharmacy, opened in the 18th century. The highlight is the recreated alchemist's lab with its replica fireplace, stove and instruments, some dating from the 16th century. There's also a display of the often stomach-turning ingredients.

➕ B7 ✉ I, Tárnok utca 18 ☎ 1 375 9772 🕐 Mar–Oct Tue–Sun 10–6; Nov–Feb Tue–Sun 10–4 🚌 16, 16A, 116 ♿ Good inside; one step outside entrance 💰 Inexpensive

BÉCSI KAPU

Vienna Gate leads into the northern end of the Castle District and is the point at which all four streets that run along the hill converge. Built originally as the start of the road linking Buda and Vienna, the medieval gate was destroyed during the siege to expel the Turks in 1686, and the one you see today was constructed in the 1930s. In the Middle Ages it was the site of a Saturday market. The square's main sights include a late 19th-century Lutheran church, the National Archives and the Museum of Military History (▷ below). You can also reach the outer walls from here, which offer views over the Buda Hills.

➕ A7 🚇 Széll Kálmán tér 🚌 16, 16A

HADTÖRTÉNETI MÚZEUM

militaria.hu

The Museum of Military History (enter on Tóth Árpád sétány, behind Bécsi kapu tér) is housed in a late 19th-century barracks. There are exhibitions on the Hungarian Hussar regiment, the 1848–49 Independence War and both world wars. One room is devoted to the 1956 Uprising, which began in Budapest and spread nationwide, but was crushed by Soviet troops.

➕ A7 ✉ I, Tóth Árpád sétány 40 ☎ 1 325 1600 🕐 Apr–Sep Tue–Sun 10–6, Oct–Mar Tue–Sun 10–4 🚇 Széll Kálmán tér 🚌 16, 116 ♿ Good 💰 Moderate

Golden Eagle Pharmacy Museum

Statue at Bécsi Kapu (Vienna Gate)

MÁRIA MAGDOLNA TEMPLOM

The bulk of the Church of Mary Magdalene was destroyed during bombing in 1944, but the tower was preserved. The 13th-century church was constructed for Hungarian residents (German settlers used the Mátyás Church).

➕ A7 ✉ I, Kapisztrán tér 6 🚇 Széll Kálmán tér 🚌 16, 16A, 116

ORSZÁGOS SZÉCHÉNYI KÖNYVTÁR

oszk.hu

The National Széchényi Library, which is now situated in the palace, was founded in 1802 by Ferenc Széchényi (father of the great reformer, István). He dreamed of making Hungary one of Europe's powerhouses of learning. There are a few Corvina codices from King Mátyás's lauded Renaissance library, some of the oldest known medieval illuminated scripts, among more than 600,000 manuscripts and 180,000 maps.

➕ B8 ✉ I, Wing F, Budavári palota ☎ 1 224 3700 🕐 Reading rooms: Tue–Sat 9–8; closed mid-Jul to mid-Aug 🍴 Café 🚌 5, 16, 16A, 116, 178 ♿ Good 💷 Inexpensive

RÉGI BUDAI VÁROSHÁZA

The former Buda town hall was built in the late 17th century before the unification of the settlements of Buda, Pest and Óbuda to form a single city. There's a statue of Pallas Athene, the Guardian of Buda, at the corner of the building.

➕ B7 ✉ Szentháromság tér 2 🚌 16, 16A, 116

SIKLÓ

If you don't fancy climbing the walkways leading up Castle Hill, take the funicular railway. Originally built in 1870, it had to be rebuilt after damage during World War II, and finally reopened in 1986.

➕ B8 ✉ I, Clark Ádám tér–Szent György tér ☎ 1 201 9128 🕐 Daily 7.30–10; closed first and third Mon of the month 🚌 16, 105; tram: 19, 41 ♿ Good 💷 Moderate

Sikló (funicular railway)

Equestrian statue outside the former town hall

Castle Walk

Take in the main sights of the Castle District and enjoy views over the Buda Hills from its fortified walls.

DISTANCE: 1.5km (1 mile) **ALLOW:** 1–1.5 hours

START

SZENT GYÖRGY TÉR
✚ B8 🚋 Sikló (funicular)

END

DÍSZ TÉR ✚ B8 🚌 16, 16A, 116;
Sikló from Szent György tér

① Take the funicular (▷ 32) from Clark Ádám tér to Szent György tér. Sándor Palace, the president's official residence, is on the right as you alight.

② Turn left and pass through the first gate into the palace complex (▷ 26), following the steps down to the river-facing terrace at the front. Turn right through the arch behind the statue of Eugene of Savoy.

③ Take a look at the Mátyás Well, turn left into the Lion Courtyard and then return to Szent György tér by the second gate (past the statue of the horseherd). Follow Szent György utca to Dísz tér.

④ Walk up Tárnok utca, past the Golden Eagle Pharmacy Museum (▷ 31) and on to Szentháromság tér. See Mátyás Church (▷ 30) and the Fishermen's Bastion (▷ 25).

⑧ Then head to the right along Úri utca, looking at the carved detail on the elegant houses. Finish at Dísz tér.

⑦ Follow the promenade that runs along the district's outer wall, past a memorial to the last Turkish governor. Tóth Árpád sétány is home to the Museum of Military History (▷ 31). Turn left on to Szentháromság utca, stopping at Ruszwurm (▷ 36).

⑥ Move left into the adjoining Kapisztrán tér, home to the single tower of the Church of Mary Magdalene (▷ 32), and then climb some steps to the right of the National Archives.

⑤ Continue up Táncsics Mihály utca until you reach Bécsi kapu tér.

Shopping

BORTÁRSASÁG

bortarsasag.hu

One of several shops operated by the Hungarian Wine Society, this store offers free wine-tasting sessions on Saturday afternoons and has a wide range of wines from all over the country.

B6 I, Batthyány utca 59 1 212 2569 Mon–Fri 10–7, Sat 10–6 11, 39

DÍSZ TÉRI PIAC

This daily outdoor market on the eastern side of Dísz tér sells handicrafts, embroidery and other traditional goods likely to appeal to the many tourists who visit the Castle District.

B8 I, Dísz tér Daily 9–7 16, 16A, 116

FÉNY UTCAI PIAC

fenyutcaipiac.hu

Situated behind Mammut (▷ this page), just off Széll Kálmán tér, this vibrant market sells an array of meat, vegetables, wines, cheeses, flowers and pickles. The stalls are outside, but are protected from the elements by a transparent roof. Prices are a little higher than some neighborhood markets, but the produce is fresh and good quality.

A6 II, Lövőház utca 12 1 345 4112 Mon–Fri 6–6, Sat 6–2 Széll Kálmán tér 5, 16, 16A, 116

LITEA

litea.hu

This diminutive shop on a back alley off Hess András tér sells books and CDs, and also has tables where you can enjoy a hot drink and write postcards (they sell the arty kind). A great place to browse and buy interesting books on Hungary (in English). You'll find the entrance to the alley on the opposite side of the road from the Hilton.

B7 I, Hess András tér 4 1 375 6987 Daily 10–6 16, 16A, 116

MAMMUT

mammut.hu

Divided between two enormous buildings either side of Lövőház utca, at the back of Széna tér (next to Széll Kálmán tér), Mammut is one of the city's leading shopping malls. As well as more than 300 shops, there are bars, nightclubs, 40 restaurants and cafés, a 13-screen cinema complex and a sporting and fitness area. It's a popular place with the city's youth.

A6 II, Lövőház utca 2–6 1 345 8020 Mon–Sat 10–9, Sun 10–6 Széll Kálmán tér Tram: 4, 6

VÁRFOK GALÉRIA

varfok-galeria.hu

Works of contemporary Hungarian art are sold from this gallery, which is a short walk from Bécsi kapu (▷ 31) to the north of the Castle District. Founded soon after the political changes in 1990, it was one of the first private contemporary art galleries in the country. Exhibitions that feature both new young talent and renowned artists often reveal exciting new trends.

A7 I, Várfok utca 11 1 213 5155 Tue–Sat 11–6 Széll Kálmán tér 16, 16A, 39, 116

ATRIUM

atriumfilmszinhaz.hu

A Bauhaus arts space with cinema, contemporary dance, live music and theatrical performances with English subtitles. There's also an art-deco café and bar in the lobby.

➕ A6 ✉ II, Margit körút 55 ☎ 1 317 9338
🕐 Daily 10am–midnight 🚇 Széll Kálmán tér
🚃 Tram: 4, 6

CAFÉ MIRÓ

cafemiro.hu

This café-bar is well positioned near Mátyás Church (▷ 30), and displays the works of artist Joan Miró. It has a vibrant atmosphere, playing contemporary music amid modern furnishings. Hungarian and international food are on the menu.

➕ A7 ✉ I, Úri utca 30 ☎ 1 201 2375
🕐 Daily 9–midnight 🚌 16, 16A, 116

MANNA

mannalounge.com

Manna—a bar and elegant restaurant playing live music in the evening—sits above the western side of the tunnel that runs through Castle Hill. There are also large video installations showing European urban scenes, and a stylish summer terrace.

➕ B8 ✉ II, Palota utca 17 ☎ 20 9999 188
🕐 Summer daily 6–1; winter Mon–Fri 12–12
🚌 5, 178

MÁTYÁS TEMPLOM

matyas-templom.hu

Throughout the year, Mátyás Church (▷ 30) is the spectacular setting for choral events, organ recitals, orchestral concerts and festivals featuring world-class musicians. The pastel-coloured stonework somehow enhances the mesmerising music.

➕ B7 ✉ I, Szentháromság tér 2 ☎ 1 489 0716 🕐 Mon–Fri 9–5, Sat 9–12, Sun 1–5
🚌 16, 16A, 116

MILLENÁRIS PARK

millenaris.hu

This cultural and recreational area in a purpose-built park behind Széll Kálmán tér has concerts and festivals. There are two indoor performance spaces and in the summer events are hosted outside.

➕ A6 ✉ II, Kis Rókus utca 16–20 ☎ 1 336 4000 🚇 Széll Kálmán tér 🚃 Tram: 4, 6

OSCAR BAR

oscarbar.hu

A basement bar a short distance outside Bécsi kapu which, as its name suggests, is devoted to the world of Hollywood film. Budapest's first American-style cocktail bar offers over 200 cocktails.

➕ A7 ✉ I, Ostrom utca 14 ☎ 30 276 3898
🕐 Wed–Thu 5pm–2am, Fri–Sat 5pm–3am
🚇 Széll Kálmán tér 🚌 16, 16A, 39, 116

NATIONAL DANCE THEATER

The National Dance Theater was founded in the 18th century in a former monastery buildin—next to the Sándor Palace—that had become redundant when József II disbanded the order. Like the Mátyás Church, it catered primarily to the significant German population that lived in the Castle District. Despite this, in 1790 it hosted the first-ever professional play performed in the Hungarian language. Its other claim to fame is that Beethoven played inside in 1800. The company moved out of the building in 2014 (so it could be used as government offices); in the future, their performances of Hungarian dance will take place in Millenáris Park, although they are temporarily using various other venues in the city.

Where to Eat

ARANY KAVIÁR (€€€)

aranykaviar.hu

Classy, intimate, fine-dining restaurant
on the road below Bécsi kapu (▷ 31)
specializing in traditional Russian cuisine
with a modern twist. You can order iced
glasses of vodka and there is a selection
of dishes featuring caviar. The *fin-de-siècle* decor creates an elegant ambience.

🞢 A7 ✉ I, Ostrom utca 19 ☎ 1 201 6737
🕑 Daily 12–2.30, 6–10.30 🚇 Széll Kálmán tér
🚌 16, 16A, 39, 116

BALTAZÁR (€€)

baltazarbudapest.com

A superb restaurant where you can
enjoy grilled dishes and Hungarian
classics in a dining room featuring
cartoon illustrations on the walls and
bare hanging lightbulbs. There's a huge
selection of wines.

🞢 A7 ✉ I, Országház utca 31 ☎ 1 300
7050 🕑 Daily 12–12 🚌 16, 16A, 116

CAFÉ CULTURE

While the Ruszwurm is the city's longest-
established café, it is far from the only one
with a distinguished history. The café or
coffeehouse played a vital social role in the
19th and early 20th centuries as a meeting
place and social forum (often for artists
and political thinkers). Many were lavishly
furnished, and some remain in the city
center today, still full of atmosphere,
including Gerbeaud, the Centrál and
the Europa.

CAFÉ PIERROT (€€€)

pierrot.hu

Family-run for over 30 years, this is a
well-regarded café and restaurant found
toward the northern end of the Castle
District. Housed in a 13th-century
bakery, it has a lovely garden terrace
and serves specialties from the
Carpathian region.

🞢 A7 ✉ I, Fortuna utca 14 ☎ 1 375 6971
🕑 Daily 12–12 🚌 16, 16A, 116

HALÁSZBÁSTYA (€€€)

halaszbastya.eu

Behind Mátyás Church (▷ 30)
and overlooking the Danube, the
Fishermen's Bastion Restaurant has
fantastic city views, especially from its
terraces. The upper Margaréta Terrace is
heated in winter and a folk band often
plays in the afternoon.

🞢 B7 ✉ I, Halászbástya-Északi Híradástorony
☎ 1 201 6935 🕑 Daily 10am–midnight
🚌 16, 16A, 116

RUSZWURM (€)

ruszwurm.hu

Ruszwurm is the oldest café (and one
of the smallest) in the city, established
in 1827, and decorated with lovely
Biedermeier furnishings. This was a
favorite place of Empress Sissi and is
still a charming place to enjoy cakes.

🞢 A7 ✉ I, Szentháromság utca 7 ☎ 1 375
5284 🕑 Daily 10–7 🚌 16, 16A, 116

SPEIZ (€€€)

speiz.hu

On Castle Hill near Mátyás Church
(▷ 30), "The Pantry" serves up traditional Hungarian flavors alongside
imaginative modern European dishes.

🞢 B7 ✉ I, Hess András tér 6 ☎ 1 488 7416
🕑 Daily 12–12 in summer; Tue–Sat 12–10,
Sun 12–5 in winter 🚌 16, 16A, 116

Gellért Hill rises to the south of Castle Hill, crowned with the Citadella and Freedom Monument. Serb immigrants settled in the area between the two hills—known as the Tabán—during the 18th century. Residential streets lead up Rose Hill to the north.

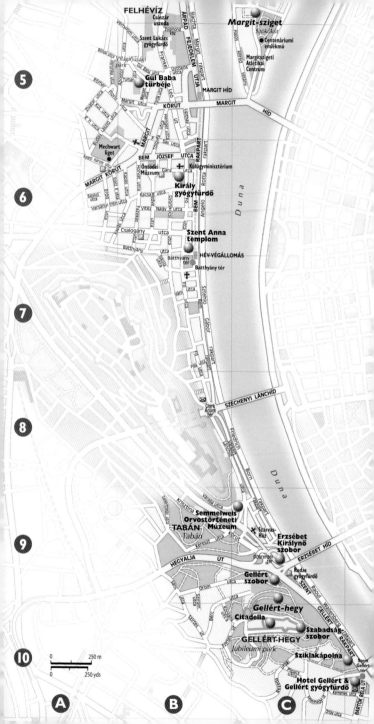

FELHÉVÍZ

Császár
uszoda

Szent Lukács
gyógyfürdő

Világifjúsági
park

**Gül Baba
türbéje**

Margit-sziget

Centenáriumi
emlékmű

Margitszigeti
Atlétikai
Centrum

MARGIT HÍD

MARGIT

KÖRÚT

5

MARGIT

ÁRPÁD FEJEDELEM ÚTJA

Mechwart
liget

MARGIT KÖRÚT

Öntödei
Múzeum

BEM   JÓZSEF   UTCA

Külügyminisztérium

**Király
gyógyfürdő**

6

Ganz

BEM

Angelo

Rotta

D u n a

**Szent Anna
templom**

Csalogány
utca

HÉV-VÉGÁLLOMÁS

Batthyány
utca

Batthyány tér

Batthyány tér

7

Szenő

Gábor

rakpart

Fő utca

Pala utca

SZÉCHENYI LÁNCHÍD

Clark Ádám tér

8

Fridrich

Bem

utca

rakpart

D u n a

Krisztina

Virália utca

**Semmelweis
Orvostörténeti
Múzeum**

TABÁN

Tabán

Szarvas-
Ház

**Erzsébet
Királynő
szobor**

9

Döbrentei tér

ERZSÉBET HÍD

HEGYALJA   ÚT

Rudas
gyógyfürdő

**Gellért
szobor**

Gellért-hegy

Citadella

**Szabadság-
szobor**

GELLÉRT-HEGY

Jubileumi park

Szíklakápolna

10

0   250 m

0   250 yds

**Hotel Gellért &
Gellért gyógyfürdő**

BARTÓK BÉLA ÚT

A   **B**   **C**

SZABADSÁG HÍD

D E F

Gellért-hegy

Stunning view of Pest and the Danube (left); Gellért Statue (right)

THE BASICS

➕ C9

🍴 Restaurant just below the citadel on Szirtes út

🚌 27 (up the hill), 7, 133E; tram: 19, 41, 47, 49 (to the base of the hill)

♿ Ascent difficult without transport

🎫 Free

HIGHLIGHTS

● Cave Chapel (▷ 46)
● Citadel (▷ 45)
● Freedom Monument—a statue of a woman holding a palm leaf above her head (▷ 46)
● Gellért Statue (▷ 45)
● The river views

If you fancy a bit of exercise, brave a walk up Gellért Hill. At its peak are a couple of the city's most recognizable landmarks—and you can take a bird's-eye view of the river below.

The name The 140m (459ft) granite hill is named after an Italian bishop who was martyred here in the 11th century. When King István decided to adopt Christianity as the state religion—in part as a means of unifying the country and dispatching rivals—he employed the services of the missionary bishop Gellért. When István died heirless, there was a power vacuum during which the unfortunate bishop was nailed inside a barrel and thrown down the hill by pagans. A statue of him (▷ 45) bearing a crucifix stands part way up the hill, directly above Elizabeth Bridge.

Getting to the top There are several ways to scale the hill's heights. There is a car park, and the No. 27 bus will carry you most of the way (catch it from Móricz Zsigmond körtér). However, if you can stand the tough walk up then you'll get the most from what the hill has to offer. Paths snake their way up its sides, and there are benches and viewing points along the way. If you start from opposite Hotel Gellért (▷ 41), visit the Cave Chapel (▷ 46) before continuing up to the top. Once there, you can walk around the citadel (▷ 45)—built by the Habsburgs to counter further rebellion after the 1848–49 Independence War.

Hotel Gellért (right) and the famous adjacent baths (left)

Hotel Gellért and Gellért gyógyfürdő

Built in the early 20th century, Hotel Gellért is among the city's best-known places to stay. The opulent baths next door are fed by thermal springs bubbling up from deep beneath Gellért Hill.

The hotel Bishop Gellért is well remembered on the Buda side of Freedom Bridge, where Gellért Hill faces Hotel Gellért and the Gellért Baths across Gellért tér. Completed in 1918 in art-nouveau style, this historic hotel, which once hosted world celebrities and heads of state, is very gradually being refurbished. Its broad, symmetrical facade looks lovely when illuminated at night and there is a porcelain fountain in front. Guests get one free entry to the adjacent baths.

The baths The impressive Gellért Baths are the most popular with tourists—and are the city's costliest. The entrance hall is adorned with bright tiles from the Zsolnay factory in Pécs and stained-glass windows depicting episodes from an epic Hungarian poem. Natural spring water heats 12 baths and pools in this fully mixed spa complex which also has an outdoor area for sunbathing (around a large pool with wave machine). On entering you buy a ticket either for a private changing cubicle or a locker in a shared area. If you choose the latter, you'll be given a tag with a number on it. Take the tag to the changing room attendant, who will open a locker for you and chalk your tag number on the inside of the door; but do make sure to remember your locker number.

THE BASICS

danubiushotels.com
gellertbath.com
✚ D10
✉ XI, Szent Gellért tér 1
☎ 1 889 5500 (hotel);
1 466 6166 (baths)
🕐 Baths: daily 6am–8pm.
Last entry 7pm
🍴 Restaurants, café, bar
🚌 7, 7A, 86; tram: 18, 19,
47; metro: Szent Gellért tér
♿ Poor but renovations
should offer easier access
💰 Baths: expensive;
prices are higher at
weekends

HIGHLIGHT

● The architecture—many tourists pop their heads in simply to admire the grand entrance hall

TIPS

● Take flip-flops.
● It is compulsory to wear a swimcap in the swimming pool.
● Book treatments in advance.

Margit-sziget

HIGHLIGHT

● Exploring the island on a *bringóhintó*—a pedal-powered buggy available to rent near the southern end

TIP

● Cars may access the island from Árpád Bridge (as far as a car park at the northern end). Only bus No. 26 runs on to the island itself.

Margaret Island—topped and tailed by the Árpád and Margit bridges—is a summer favorite with Budapest residents, who come here to swim, cycle, stroll or just laze about on the grass while enjoying the sun.

The history Known as the Island of Hares in Roman times, Margaret Island may then have been a retreat for lepers (the Latin words for hare and leper being similar). Later it was the site of a Turkish pasha's harem and enjoyed a soft spot in the heart of Palatine Ferenc I, who planted rare trees during the late 18th century. The current name is a reminder of its more sober history as a hub of monasticism; following the Mongol invasion of 1241–42, King Béla IV promised his next-born would spend a life of

religious devotion in return for God's future protection of Hungary. He was true to his word, and his famously pious daughter, Margit, lived on the island. Writers and artists flocked here during the 19th century to take advantage of the medicinal waters in a bathing hall designed by architect Miklós Ybl.

The sights You can walk on to the island from Margaret Bridge. Look for the Palatinus Swimming Baths, which boast several pools and water slides; the remains of a medieval Franciscan church and the foundations of the Dominican church and cloister built for Margit; an art-nouveau water tower lookout and the Japanese garden. The rebuilt Premonstratensian chapel originally dated to the 11th to 12th centuries and is the city's earliest structure.

THE BASICS

➕ C4

🍴 Restaurant, café (Danubius Health Spa Resort); restaurant (Danubius Grand Hotel Margitsziget)

🚌 26, 34, 106; tram: 4, 6

📅 Daily in summer

♿ Free

More to See

CITADELLA
citadella.hu

The citadel at the top of Gellért Hill was built by the Habsburgs (after the failed uprising in 1848–49) as a deterrent to future rebellion. There are two exhibitions; one about the history of the area, the other about a World War II bunker.

➕ C10 🍴 Restaurant and café 🚌 27 ♿ Good (approach from back of the hill) 💰 Inexpensive/moderate (access to history/bunker exhibitions)

ERZSÉBET KIRÁLYNŐ SZOBOR

A bronze statue of the 19th-century Austrian Empress Erzsébet—known as Sissi—sits just to the north of Elizabeth Bridge. Sissi was assassinated by an anarchist in 1898. She was known for immersing herself into Hungarian culture.

➕ C9 ✉ I, Döbrentei tér 🚌 5, 7, 8, 112; tram: 19, 41

GELLÉRT SZOBOR

A staggered path behind Elizabeth Bridge leads up to a waterfall and statue of Gellért. The bishop was the right-hand man of King István and tutor to his son, and was gruesomely murdered here in 1046 after the king's death.

➕ C9 ✉ XI, Gellért-hegy 🚌 5, 7, 8, 112; tram: 19, 41

GÜL BABA TÜRBÉJE

At the top of Rózsadomb is the 16th-century tomb of Gül Baba, a Turkish dervish who lived on the hill. He is said to have grown flowers and became known as the "Father of Roses."

➕ B5 ✉ II, Mecset utca 14 ☎ 1 237 4400 🕐 Daily 10–6 🍴 Café next door 🚌 91, 191, 291; tram: 4, 6, 17 ♿ None (and there are several sets of stairs, which makes access difficult) 💰 Free

KIRÁLY GYÓGYFÜRDŐ
kiralyfurdo.hu

The 16th-century Király (King) Baths have an original Turkish cupola (open to men and women). Visitors can enjoy four thermal baths and various massage treatments.

Bronze statue of Empress Erzsébet (above)

Freedom Monument (opposite)

Tomb of Gül Baba (right)

🚩 B6 ✉ II, Fő utca 84 ☎ 1 202 3688
🕑 Daily 9–9 (mixed at all times) 🚌 9, 109;
tram: 19 ♿ None 💰 Moderate

SEMMELWEIS ORVOSTÖRTÉNETI MÚZEUM

semmelweis.museum.hu

Ignác Semmelweis (1818–65) was a Hungarian physician who discovered the link between deaths in childbirth and poor hospital hygiene. He is now known as an early pioneer of antiseptic procedures. The house where he was born contains a history of medicine.

🚩 C9 ✉ I, Apród utca 1–3 ☎ 1 375 3533
🕑 Mar–Oct Tue–Sun 10–6; Nov–Feb Tue–Fri 10–4, Sat–Sun 10–6 🚌 5, 178; tram: 19, 41
♿ None (museum is upstairs on the first floor) 💰 Inexpensive

SZABADSÁG-SZOBOR

The Freedom Monument was created for Admiral Horthy as a tribute to his son (who died during World War II). When the Russians "liberated" the city, however, they placed the palm of victory in the hands of the female figure, and it later became a taunting symbol of Communist oppression.

🚩 C10 ✉ XI, Gellért-hegy 🚌 27

SZENT ANNA TEMPLOM

The baroque St. Anna Church was commissioned by the Jesuits in 1740, but circumstances—including the dissolution of the Jesuit order—meant it wasn't consecrated for another 65 years.

🚩 B6 ✉ I, Batthyány tér 7 ☎ 1 201 6364
🚇 Batthyány tér 🚌 11, 39, 109; tram: 19, 41
♿ None ❓ Regular concerts

SZIKLAKÁPOLNA

The Cave Chapel opposite the Gellért Baths was built in 1926 for the Pauline order. Its entrance was walled up during the Communist period, when those connected with the monasteries were persecuted and many of the monks killed.

🚩 D10 ✉ XI, Gellért-hegy 🕑 Mon–Sat 9.30–7.30 (but closed to non-observants during Mass) 🚌 7; tram: 19, 41, 47, 49; metro: Szent Gellért tér ♿ None 💰 Free

St. Anna Church

Király Thermal Baths

This walk allows you to explore Margaret Island and the main sights of the Víziváros (Water Town) along the river bank.

DISTANCE: 6km (4 miles) **ALLOW:** 2–3 hours

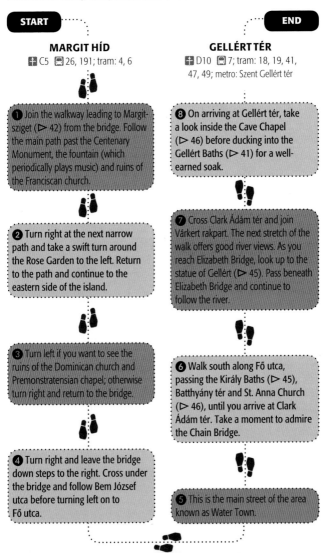

START

MARGIT HÍD
🔲 C5 🚌 26, 191; tram: 4, 6

❶ Join the walkway leading to Margit-sziget (▷ 42) from the bridge. Follow the main path past the Centenary Monument, the fountain (which periodically plays music) and ruins of the Franciscan church.

❷ Turn right at the next narrow path and take a swift turn around the Rose Garden to the left. Return to the path and continue to the eastern side of the island.

❸ Turn left if you want to see the ruins of the Dominican church and Premonstratensian chapel; otherwise turn right and return to the bridge.

❹ Turn right and leave the bridge down steps to the right. Cross under the bridge and follow Bem József utca before turning left on to Fő utca.

END

GELLÉRT TÉR
🔲 D10 🚌 7; tram: 18, 19, 41, 47, 49; metro: Szent Gellért tér

❽ On arriving at Gellért tér, take a look inside the Cave Chapel (▷ 46) before ducking into the Gellért Baths (▷ 41) for a well-earned soak.

❼ Cross Clark Ádám tér and join Várkert rakpart. The next stretch of the walk offers good river views. As you reach Elizabeth Bridge, look up to the statue of Gellért (▷ 45). Pass beneath Elizabeth Bridge and continue to follow the river.

❻ Walk south along Fő utca, passing the Király Baths (▷ 45), Batthyány tér and St. Anna Church (▷ 46), until you arrive at Clark Ádám tér. Take a moment to admire the Chain Bridge.

❺ This is the main street of the area known as Water Town.

Entertainment and Nightlife

A38

a38.hu

The A38 has developed into a popular venue. Unusually, it is an ex-industrial ship that was brought from Ukraine, and is moored permanently on the Buda bank near Petőfi Bridge. Along with hosting live-music events, it has a restaurant and nightclub, five bars and an exhibition space.

🞖 E11 ✉ Petőfi híd ☎ 1 464 3940 🚌 103, 212; tram: 4, 6

CAFÉ DEL RIO

rio.hu

Local and international DJs play dance and Latino-style music at this well-established waterside outdoor club.

🞖 E11 ✉ XI, Hengermalom utca ☎ 20 779 3311 🕐 May–Sep daily 8pm–5am (closed Oct–Apr) 🚌 33, 103; tram: 1

RUDAS ROMKERT

romkert.eu

A buzzing atmosphere during the summer months make this paved terrace outside the Rudas Baths a good spot for a coffee during the day and a dance at night.

🞖 C9 ✉ XI, Döbrentei tér 9 ☎ 30 540 6991 🕐 May–Sep Tue–Sat noon–5am, Sun–Mon noon–8 (closed rest of year) 🚌 5, 7, 8; tram: 19, 41

BARBA NEGRA TRACK

barbanegra.hu

A fun summer music venue below the Rákóczi Bridge on the Buda bridgehead. The shows include affordable concerts featuring Hungarian artists.

🞖 E11 ✉ XI, Neumann János utca 2 ☎ 20 563 2254 🕐 May–Sep daily 9pm–6am (closed rest of year) 🚌 153; tram: 4, 6

Where to Eat

PRICES
Prices are approximate, based on a 3-course meal for one person.
€€€   over 7,000Ft
€€   4,000–7,000Ft
€   under 4,000Ft

BÚSULÓ JUHÁSZ (€€€)

busulojuhasz.hu

An atmospheric restaurant below the citadel, with a tiered terrace and views of the Buda Hills. It specializes in traditional Hungarian cuisine elegantly presented, and offers a good wine list.

🞖 B10 ✉ XI, Kelenhegyi út 58 ☎ 1 209 1649 🕐 Daily 12–12 🚌 27

MARGITKERT (€–€€)

margitkert.com

Best known for the live music of Gyula Horváth, the leading violinist of the Budapest Gypsy Symphony Orchestra. The Hungarian cuisine is filling.

🞖 B5 ✉ II, Margit utca 15 ☎ 1 326 0860 🕐 Daily 12–12 🚌 91; tram: 4, 6

TRÓFEA GRILL (€–€€)

trofeagrill.eu

Fixed-price all-you-can-eat buffet featuring traditional Hungarian food. The prices include drinks and live music.

🞖 B5 ✉ II, Margit körút 2 ☎ 1 438 9090 🕐 Mon–Fri 12–12, Sat 11.30–9 🚌 5, 91, 191; tram: 4, 6, 17

It is in the area known as **Leopold Town** that the city's main financial, legal and spiritual strands meet. Here you'll find not only the Parliament building, but also St. Stephen's Basilica, home to the country's most holy relic.

Magyar Állami Operaház

TOP 25

The grand State Opera House was constructed in the 19th century

THE BASICS

opera.hu
* D7
* VI, Andrássy út 22
* 1 332 9714
* Guided tours (in English) daily at 3 and 4. Groups by appointment
* 1 332 8197
* Opera
* 105; trolley-bus: 70, 78
* Good (but call in advance to arrange a tour)
* Guided tour: expensive

DID YOU KNOW?

● The auditorium holds nearly 1,300 spectators.
● During restoration in the 1990s, 300,000 pieces of gold leaf were used in replacing the gilding.
● The auditorium's chandelier weighs more than two tons.

The Budapest State Opera House is one of the most sumptuous buildings in the capital. Tickets are excellent value, but even if you don't take in a performance it's well worth a peek inside.

Size isn't everything When Ferenc József agreed to fund the construction of the opera house he ordered that it be smaller than its equivalent in Vienna. Miklós Ybl followed his wishes to the letter, but he succeeded in upstaging the Austrian capital in another way: the (probably fanciful) story goes that when the emperor saw the finished building he regretted he hadn't mentioned that it should also be less beautiful. Ybl was painstakingly meticulous and the building process took nearly a decade. Ferenc Erkel, the father of Hungarian opera and composer of the national anthem, conducted two of his creations (*Bánk Bán* and *Hunyadi László*) on the opening day in 1884. Among big names to have served as director are Gustav Mahler and Otto Klemperer.

The decoration On approaching the neo-Renaissance building you'll see statues of Ferenc Erkel and Ferenc Liszt either side of the entrance, as well as the figures of other great composers (including Beethoven and Mozart) above the balcony on the first floor. Inside is a grand staircase leading to the auditorium, which is painted in rich red and gilded with gold leaf. The frescoes are by leading historicist artists Károly Lotz, Bertalan Székely and Mór Than.

LIPÓTVÁROS TOP 25

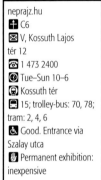

The Museum of Ethnography often gets overlooked, but it's one of the city's most vibrant collections. The permanent exhibition is devoted to traditional dress and crafts, and there are frequent interesting temporary displays.

The history The story behind the birth of the building is an interesting one. In the 1880s, a competition was held to design the Parliament building, which was being erected to coincide with the millennial celebrations of 1896. Imre Steindl was the winner, but the runner-up designs weren't wasted: two of them were also constructed on Kossuth tér to house political and legal bodies—including this building by Alajos Hauszmann, which held the Supreme Court for half a century.

The exhibition There's a certain mismatch between the high-blown nature of the building and the more earthy, local items it holds. Many of these were gathered during a period of obsession with national identity (and, by extension, traditional and folkloric arts and crafts) that emerged in the late 19th century. Thirteen rooms on the first floor hold objects relating to the life of the peasantry between the 18th century and World War I, including working tools, decorated furniture, everyday dress and festival costumes. There are also reconstructions of peasant houses from Transdanubia, as well as old film clips, photographs, manuscripts and sound recordings.

THE BASICS

neprajz.hu

🔍 C6

✉ V, Kossuth Lajos tér 12

☎ 1 473 2400

🕐 Tue–Sun 10–6

🚇 Kossuth tér

🚌 15; trolley-bus: 70, 78; tram: 2, 4, 6

♿ Good. Entrance via Szalay utca

🎫 Permanent exhibition: inexpensive

HIGHLIGHTS

● Interior of early 19th-century peasant house from the Őrség region
● Decorated 19th-century kitchen from a rich farmhouse in the Sárköz region

---

LIPÓTVÁROS TOP 25

53

Országház

You're unlikely to miss the looming Parliament building, which dominates the Pest bank at Kossuth tér. Inside is the national symbol—the Holy Crown.

The background Imre Steindl's neo-Gothic creation was the winner in the competition to build Parliament, the main project of several commissioned to coincide with the 1,000th anniversary of the Magyar arrival. Steindl was slightly lucky to have the opportunity—a previous competition in the 1840s had been won by Frigyes Feszl, but the 1848–49 Independence War meant the project never got off the ground. The influence of the Houses of Parliament in London is obvious in the thin, pinnacled spires, but Steindl also introduced a round baroque central hall and a dome.

The baroque dome of the Parliament (left); the lavish interior (right)

The interior On entering the building, you pass into a hall with eight enormous marble pillars. A sweeping staircase leads up to the main hall beneath the dome—look up to frescoes by Károly Lotz. The stained-glass windows that frame the space are by Miksa Róth. Of the two near-identical chambers, only that to the south (the Chamber of Representatives) is used for parliamentary business.

Crowning glory In the middle of the Dome Hall stands a case containing the Holy Crown, scepter, orb and sword. The crown, with its bent cross, is the primary feature of the country's coat of arms, and can be seen on the national flag. Tradition states that this was the crown given to King István in AD1000 by the Pope, but it actually dates from the 12th century.

THE BASICS

parliament.hu
+ C6
✉ V, Kossuth Lajos tér 1–3
☎ 1 441 4904
🕐 Guided tours only. In English daily at 10, 12, 1, 2, 3. Tours last about 45 minutes
🚇 Kossuth tér
🚌 15, 115; trolley-bus: 70, 78; tram: 2
♿ Good (but telephone at least two days in advance to arrange assistance)
💷 Expensive for non-EU citizens, moderate for EU citizens

Szent István Bazilika

TOP
25

HIGHLIGHTS

● Views from the Panorama Tower
● Right hand of St. Stephen

TIP

● The Basilica hosts organ concerts every Monday at 5pm (7pm in October), as well as Friday at 8pm between April and December. For program details, see www.organconcert.hu.

St. Stephen's Basilica is the capital's largest church—although only the third-biggest in the country as a whole—and home to the Holy Right, the country's most sacred relic.

A troubled history The Basilica had difficult beginnings. It was originally designed by József Hild, who died in 1867 not only before his neo-classical creation was completed but before it collapsed (apparently because of low-grade building materials). Miklós Ybl took over the project, and conceived a neo-Renaissance church with a dome measuring 96m (315ft) in height—a conscious nod to the time of the Magyar arrival in AD896. He, too, died before the building was finished in 1906. There was extensive fire damage during World War II and

Clockwise from left: The grand facade of St. Stephen's Basilica; an altar painting of Stephen offering his crown to the Virgin by Gyula Benczúr; the magnificent dome; detail of wooden and brass doors; entrance archway to the basilica

restorations weren't finalized until 50 years later. The church interior takes the shape of a Greek cross, its floor laid with slabs of black and white marble. There is a fine statue of St. Stephen by Alajos Stróbl on the high altar, while the dome is decorated with mosaics by Károly Lotz.

Take in the sights The object of most interest, within the church, is the mummified right hand of St. Stephen himself, the founder of the Christian state. The hand is held in a precious casket, and is illuminated on payment of a coin. The Panorama Tower—an exterior gallery running around the base of the dome—offers lovely city views. You can climb steps the whole distance to the gallery or take a lift two-thirds of the way.

THE BASICS

basilica.hu
D7
V, Szent István tér
1 311 0839
Mon–Fri 9–5,
Sat 9–1, Sun 1–5
Bajcsy Zsilinszky utca,
Deák tér, Arany János
utca
15; trolley-bus: 70, 72,
73, 78
Good
Church: free; treasury,
Panorama Tower:
inexpensive
Guided tours available

More to See

CIPÖK A DUNA-PARTON

North of the Chain Bridge, 60 pairs of iron shoes lie on the river bank. This sculpture commemorates the murder of Jews here by Arrow Cross militia in 1944–45.

🞦 C7 ⊠ Along Antall József Rakpart 🚇 Kossuth tér 🚊 15; trolley-bus: 70, 78; tram: 2

KOSSUTH LAJOS TÉR

Kossuth tér holds the Parliament building and is named after the leader of the 1848 uprising against Habsburg rule. An eternal flame commemorates the victims of the notorious 1956 Uprising, which was suppressed by Soviet tanks.

🞦 C6 🚇 Kossuth tér 🚊 15; trolley-bus: 70, 78; tram: 2 ♿ Good

MAGYAR TUDOMÁNYOS AKADÉMIA

mta.hu

The Hungarian Academy of Sciences is housed in a neo-Renaissance palace, and was founded by the great reformer István Széchenyi in the early 19th century. There is a small collection of art that visitors can see Monday–Friday 11–4.

🞦 C7 ⊠ V, Széchenyi István tér 9 ☎ 1 411 6100 🚇 Kossuth tér, Vörösmarty tér 🚊 15, 16; tram: 2

NYUGATI PÁLYAUDVAR

The Western Railway Station was the city's first. It was completed in 1877 and was designed by the company run by Gustave Eiffel (of Eiffel Tower fame).

🞦 D6 ⊠ VI, Teréz körút 55–57 🍽 Restaurant and café 🚇 Nyugati pályaudvar 🚊 6, 26, 91, 191; trolley-bus: 72, 73; tram: 4, 6

SZABADSÁG TÉR

Freedom Square was the place where leading rebels against Habsburg rule (including Lajos Batthyány, prime minister during the 1848–49 Independence War) were executed in 1849; the Eternal Light burns in remembrance.

🞦 C7 🚇 Kossuth tér 🚊 15; trolley-bus: 70, 78; tram: 2

Soviet Memorial on Szabadság tér

AJKA KRISTÁLY

ajka-crystal.hu

This is an outlet selling the famous Ajka crystal products. Choose from delightful gifts from glasses to vases, bowls and decanters.

🔲 D6 ⊠ XIII, Szent István körút 18 ☎ 1 340 5083 🕓 Mon–Fri 10–6, Sat 10–1 🚇 Nyugati pályaudvar 🚋 Tram: 2, 4, 6

ANDRÁSSY ÚT

The first section of the city's main avenue is dotted with designer shops along its way, including clothes boutiques and upscale stores selling crystal, porcelain, leather goods and jewelry.

🔲 D8–E6 ⊠ VI, Andrássy út 🕓 Shops generally open Mon–Fri 10–6, Sat 10–2 🚇 Oktogon, Opera, Bajcsy-Zsilinszky út

FALK MIKSA UTCA

Running north from Kossuth tér as far as Szent István körút, this street holds the best of Budapest's antiques shops. There are dozens of stores along its length, selling furniture, art, oriental crafts, jewelry and porcelain.

🔲 C6 🕓 Shops generally Mon–Fri 10–6, Sat 10–2 🚇 Kossuth tér; tram: 2, 4, 6

BULL'S BLOOD

One of Hungary's most famous wines is called Bull's Blood (Bikavér), produced in Szekszárd and Eger. Its name dates to the famous siege of Eger Castle in 1552. A small number of Hungarian soldiers succeeded in repelling a Turkish force 40 times larger. They drank red wine to steel their nerves, but from a distance the Turks became convinced it was bull's blood—and that this was the secret behind their apparently superhuman strength and bravery. A deep ruby red in color, it has a subtle spicy flavor.

LEHEL CSARNOK

You won't miss this market in its bright building designed to look like a ship. It sells fresh food, traditional Hungarian produce and wines. Go to the upper level for cafés, bars and a post office.

🔲 D5 ⊠ XIII, Váci út 9–15 ☎ 1 288 6898 🕓 Mon–Fri 6–6, Sat 6–2, Sun 6–1 🚇 Lehel tér 🚌 15; trolley-bus: 76; tram: 14

MACIMŰVEK

macimuvek.hu

A family-run business that sells a varied range of teddy bears, and even offers courses on how to make your own.

🔲 D6 ⊠ XIII, Szent István körút 24 ☎ 20 993 9193 🕓 Mon–Fri 10–5 🚇 Nyugati pályaudvar 🚋 Tram: 2, 4, 6

PÁRISI NAGYÁRUHÁZ

When the Paris Department Store opened in 1909 it catered for the city's elite. Today the beautifully restored art-nouveau building houses the flagship Alexandra Books on the ground floor. Upstairs the ballroom-like Lotz Hall, adorned with Károly Lotz's amazing painted ceiling frescoes, mirrors and chandeliers, is the Bookshop Café (Lotz terem).

🔲 E7 ⊠ VI, Andrássy út 39 ☎ 1 461 5835 🕓 Daily 10–8 🚇 Opera 🚋 Tram: 4, 6

SZENT ISTVÁN TÉR

The square in front of St. Stephen's Basilica (▷ 56–57) has a couple of gift shops. Items for sale include embroidered tablecloths and other handcrafted goods. It also contains a Christmas market in December, with booths selling handicrafts and warming mulled wine.

🔲 D7 🕓 Shops generally Mon–Fri 10–6, Sat 10–2 🚇 Arany János utca 🚌 Trolley-bus: 72, 73

LIPÓTVÁROS SHOPPING

Entertainment and Nightlife

360 BAR

360bar.hu

This atmospheric roof terrace bar sits atop the art-nouveau Párisi Nagyáruház (▷ 59), and offers views over the Basilica. There's a wide range of cocktails and other drinks, and a food menu including pasta dishes and tasty quesadillas.

🔒 E7 ✉ VI, Andrássy út 39 ☎ 70 259 5153 🕙 Mon–Wed 2–12, Thu–Sat 2–2, Sun 12–12 🚇 Oktogon 🚌 105; tram: 4, 6; trolley-bus: 70, 78

BOUTIQ'BAR

boutiqbar.hu

With a sultry and sexy atmosphere, this popular cocktail bar offers imaginative drinks concocted by top-class mixologists and passionate staff.

🔒 E8 ✉ VI, Paulay Ede utca 5 ☎ 30 554 2323 🕙 Tue–Thu 6–1, Fri–Sat 6–2 🚇 Bajcsy-Zsilinszky utca 🚌 105

INSTANT

instant.co.hu

A labyrinth in two former tenements, this ruin pub (▷ 71) claims to be the biggest in the city. Complete with some crazy decor, Instant combines a gallery,

café and general cultural hub and drinking place. Check out the upside down room, the blue fish and the music.

🔒 D7 ✉ VI, Nagymező utca 38 ☎ 1 311 0704 🕙 Daily 4–3 🚇 Opera 🚌 105; trolley-bus: 70, 78

LAS VEGAS CASINO

lasvegascasino.hu

You can gamble the night away in this casino in the Sofitel Budapest Hotel, near the Chain Bridge.

🔒 C8 ✉ V, Széchenyi István tér 2 ☎ 1 317 6022 🕙 Daily 24 hours 🚌 15, 16, 105; tram: 2

MAGYAR ÁLLAMI OPERHÁZ

opera.hu

The Hungarian State Opera House looks beautiful in itself (▷ 52), but it's worth hearing a performance and enjoying the superb acoustics. The tickets are extremely cheap by Western standards.

🔒 D7 ✉ VI, Andrássy út 22 ☎ 1 353 0170 🕙 Performances Tue–Sun (closed Mon); ticket office open until 5 (or start of performance) 🚇 Opera 🚌 105; trolley-bus 70, 78

MORRISON'S OPERA

morrisons.hu

This popular pub near the Opera House (▷ 52) has two dance floors and karaoke nights. A younger crowd packs out its sister bar, Morrison's, at Szent István körút 11.

🔒 D7 ✉ VI, Révay utca 25 ☎ 1 269 4060 🕙 Daily 8–4 🚇 Opera 🚌 105; trolley-bus 70, 78

MŰVÉSZ CINEMA

artmozi.hu

The "Artist" cinema shows popular and cult films. Small stalls in the lobby also sell CDs, books and jewelry.

DUNA PALOTA

Home of the Danube Symphony Orchestra, the neo-baroque Danube Palace at Zriny utca 5, just behind the Gresham Palace (▷ 58) opened in 1885 as a palace of culture, supporting young artists. Bartók, Kodály and Dvorák played in its concert hall. It hosts art exhibitions, receptions, recitals and, between May and October, weekly performances by the Danube Folk Ensemble, talented dancers and musicians who interpret traditional Hungarian folk dances and folk music.

🚩 D6 ⊠ VI, Teréz körút 30 ☎ 1 459 5050
🕐 Daily screenings 🚇 Oktogon 🚌 105;
tram: 4, 6

NEW ORLEANS JAZZ CLUB
neworleans.hu

This smooth club hosts good live jazz
Tuesday and Wednesday; performances
generally start at around 9pm.
🚩 D7 ⊠ VI, Lovag utca 5 ☎ 30 185 5006
🕐 Daily 6pm–2am 🚌 Trolley-bus: 70, 78

OPERETTSZÍNHÁZ
operett.hu

This is the leading spot to take in a light
musical. The art-nouveau decor is

impressive and there are English
subtitles for some of the performances.
🚩 D7 ⊠ VI, Nagymező utca 17 ☎ 1
312 4866 🕐 Performances daily 🚇 Opera
🚌 105; trolley-bus: 70, 78

ÖTKERT
otkert.hu

This relaxed gastrobar with a terrace and
patio attracts the crowds on hot summer nights. It has a dance floor with DJs
and live music featuring young artists
alongside the best Hungarian bands.
🚩 C8 ⊠ V, Zrinyi utca 4 ☎ 70 330 8652
🕐 Daily noon–4am 🚇 Vörösmarty tér 🚌 16,
105; tram: 2

Where to Eat

CAFÉ KÖR (€€)
cafekor.ishosting.hu

Bistro-style Café Kör serves lighter takes
on Hungarian classic dishes, as well as
international choices. Given the quality,
the food is well priced. Its location near
St. Stephen's Basilica (▷ 56) makes it
popular with both locals and visitors,
and reserving a table here is recommended. Take cash with you as card
payments aren't possible.
🚩 D7 ⊠ V, Sas utca 17 ☎ 1 311 0053
🕐 Mon–Sat 10–10 🚇 Arany János utca
🚌 15, 115; trolley-bus: 72, 73

CALLAS (€€€)
callascafe.hu

This elegant café and restaurant
housed in a 19th century building and
next to the Opera House is popular
with those attending performances
here and at other venues in the theater
district. Stylish and precise dishes are
served all day. Live salon music is
played between 8 and 11.30pm every
evening except Monday. It has also
recently expanded by opening some
very stylish guest rooms and suites

ETIQUETTE

Dining in Hungary is generally a fairly
informal affair. Gundel (▷ 98) and the
Michelin-starred Onyx (▷ 82) are the
exceptions rather than the rule in specifying
a dress code. Do bear in mind that chic
bars attract fashionably dressed clientele.

above the café, meaning opera lovers have very little distance to travel.

➕ D7 ✉ VI, Andrássy út 20 ☎ 1 354 0954 🕐 Daily 10am–midnight 🚇 Opera 🚌 105; trolley-bus: 70, 78

EURÓPA KÁVÉHÁZ (€–€€)

europakavehaz.hu

This graceful coffeehouse beside the Vígszínház serves a wide selection of traditional pastries and desserts, as well as lighter cakes. It also offers sandwiches and salads, and there's an adjacent, less expensive pâtisserie.

➕ D5 ✉ V, Szent István körút 7–9 ☎ 1 312 2362 🕐 Daily 8.30–8 🚌 91, 191; tram: 4, 6

KÉT SZERECSEN (€€)

ketszerecsen.hu

This atmospheric restaurant—the Two Saracens—near the theaters on Nagymező utca offers good people-watching tables and tasty Mediterranean bistro-style dishes. It's also open daily for breakfast.

➕ D7 ✉ VI, Nagymező utca 14 ☎ 1 343 1984 🕐 Mon–Fri 8am–midnight, Sat–Sun 9am–midnight 🚇 Opera 🚌 105; trolley-bus: 70, 78

KISPIAC BISZTRO (€€)

kispiac.hu

Hearty, filling, home-cooked-style traditional dishes are served here. The emphasis is on pork, chicken and duck, and ingredients are sourced from the local market.

➕ D7 ✉ V, Hold utca 13 ☎ 30 430 0142 🕐 Mon–Sat 12–10 🚇 Arany János utca 🚌 15

KOLLÁZS BRASSERIE (€€€)

fourseasons.com/budapest

The restaurant of the luxurious Four Seasons Hotel is deliberately informal and specializes in blending Hungarian and international flavours. Sunday brunch is a good choice. Its position affords pleasant views across Széchenyi István tér to the river.

➕ C8 ✉ V, Széchenyi István tér 5–6 ☎ 268 6000 🕐 Mon–Sat 6–10.30, 12–10.30 🚌 16, 105; tram: 2

MAK BISZTRO (€€€)

mak.hu

Mak collects plaudits and awards for its stylish food and laid-back atmosphere. Talented chefs rely on fresh seasonal ingredients for their innovative dishes, all elegantly presented. The set lunch menu is great value.

➕ D7 ✉ V, Vigyázó Ferenc utca 4 ☎ 30 723 9383 🕐 Tue–Sat 12–3, 6–12 🚇 Arany János utca 🚌 15

PESTI DISZNO (€€)

pestidiszno.hu

Pork from the tasty mangalitsa breed of Hungarian pig features strongly on the menu of this gastro bar that also serves lighter traditional dishes, tapas style.

➕ D7 ✉ VI, Nagymező utca 19 ☎ 1 951 4061 🕐 Mon–Fri 11–11, Sat–Sun 12–12 🚇 Opera 🚌 105; trolley-bus: 70, 78

GOULASH

The dish for which Hungary is famous around the world is, of course, goulash—or, more properly, *gulyás* (pronounced goo-yash). Strictly a soup rather than a stew (a stew is called *pörkölt*), it was the traditional fare of herders (*gulyás* means cattle herder) on the plains who cooked the dish in large kettle cauldrons. It is usually made of beef, peppers, paprika, onions, potatoes and caraway seeds, and is mildly spicy (and it is not as fiery as many expect). Veal, pork or lamb are also used to make this dish.

The Belváros—or inner city—is Pest's focal point. It falls within District V and is largely contained by the river on its western side and the Small Boulevard (Kiskörút), which arcs from Széchenyi lánchíd to Szabadság híd.

Danube Boat Trip

There are up to eight cruises a day and three each evening during high season

THE BASICS

legenda.hu
+ C8
⊠ Boats depart from
Vigadó tér, pier 7
☎ 1 317 2203
🔘 *Duna Bella* during the
day, *Duna Legenda* in
the evening. For timetable
details, visit the website
🔘 Vörösmarty tér
🚊 Tram: 2
♿ Good
💰 Expensive

HIGHLIGHT

● The illuminations during
an evening cruise—
particularly the bridges,
Parliament and palace

TIP

● The evening option lasts
an hour, while you can
choose between one- and
two-hour tours during the
day (the latter including a
stop-off for a walk on
Margaret Island).

The Danube is the city's life blood, and many of the best sights are ranged along each of its banks. A boat trip is a good way to get the most from the riverscape—itself a UNESCO World Heritage Site.

The options The company Legenda offers two standard tours (daytime and evening) aboard its sightseeing boats the *Duna Bella* and *Duna Legenda*. Passengers listen to an audioguide commentary (available in 30 languages). The boats depart from a pier at Vigadó tér, heading north up to (and, during the day, around) Margaret Island before moving southward again as far as Petőfi Bridge and back to their starting point.

What you'll see On leaving Vigadó tér, you'll move beneath the Chain Bridge and on past the Academy of Sciences and Parliament on your right before reaching Margaret Island. On the way back down, look out for the spire of the Calvinist church on the western bank and behind that, on Castle Hill, Mátyás Church and the turrets of the Fishermen's Bastion. Once back under the Chain Bridge, look up to Buda Castle Palace and then the Gellért Statue looming over Elizabeth Bridge. At the other side of the bridge is the Inner City Parish Church. The Rudas Baths appear next on your right, while at the top of Gellért Hill is the Freedom Monument and Citadel. After passing the Géllert Hotel the boat will return home.

Iparművészeti Múzeum

The ceiling in the entrance hall (left); beautiful Zsolnay tiling (right)

The building containing the Museum of Applied Arts is arguably more of a draw than its collections. It represents a leading example of Secessionist architecture, and is a celebration of this turn-of-the-20th-century style.

The building Budapest's Museum of Applied Arts was only the third of its kind in Europe, its collection originally based upon purchases of industrial items for display at Vienna's World Exhibition of 1873. In 1890 a competition was opened for architects to design a dedicated building for the museum as part of the 1896 millennial celebrations. The winners were Ödön Lechner and Gyula Pártos, and the final result is regarded as a masterpiece of Lechner's lifelong dedication to creating a style uniquely Hungarian. On completion, there was widespread outrage at its extravagance and, particularly, criticism of its use of Eastern themes (which drew upon contemporary theories about Hungarians having Indian ancestry). The design blends folksy, Islamic and Hindu motifs, and makes extensive use of glazed Zsolnay ceramics.

The exhibits The Esterházy Treasury, contains artefacts from the wealthy aristocratic family. These sit alongside other permanent and temporary exhibitions that include antiques and art-nouveau furniture and furnishings, ceramics, textiles, glass, silver and prints over three floors.

THE BASICS

imm.hu

✚ E10

✉ IX, Üllői út 33–37

☎ 1 456 5107

🕙 Tue–Sun 10–6

Ⓖ Corvin-negyed

🚌 15, 115; tram: 4, 6

♿ Good; enter via Hőgyes Endre utca

✋ Prices vary according to exhibition (moderate–expensive)

HIGHLIGHTS

● The Zsolnay majolica features that decorate the walls of the museum's portico

● The striking domed roof, its Zsolnay tiles—in a diamond pattern of green and gold—visible from afar

Magyar Nemzeti Múzeum

HIGHLIGHTS

● The Hungarian coronation mantle
● Mosaic floor excavated from a Roman villa in western Hungary (the Roman lapidarium)
● 18th-century woven wall hanging depicting the liberation of Buda (room 8)

TIP

● Be sure to take a look at the fabulous allegorical and historical paintings (by 19th-century painters Mór Than and Károly Lotz) on the walls and ceiling of the main staircase.

The Hungarian National Museum is the largest in the country. The exhibits are fascinating, among them the coronation cloak of King Stephen I.

History Housed in a neoclassical pile designed by Mihály Pollack and completed in 1847, the museum was brought into being by the great reformer Ferenc Széchényi. In the early years of the 19th century, the count donated his vast collection of prints, manuscripts, books and maps to the country, and these became the core of the museum's holdings. The grounds form the backdrop to the annual Independence Day celebrations on 15 March. It was from the museum steps here on that day in 1848 that poet Sándor Petőfi addressed a crowd with his *National Song*, exhorting

A skeleton of an elephant (left) is just one of the exhibits in the Hungarian National Museum (below left and right)

Hungarians to throw off the grip of their Habsburg rulers. This was one of the sparks for the Independence War of 1848–49, in which the Habsburgs eventually proved victorious. Petőfi himself was killed during battle the following year.

The exhibitions Among the permanent exhibitions are a Roman lapidarium and a display of medieval stone sculptures in the basement level. On the ground floor—to the left of the entrance hall—is the museum's prize exhibit. The coronation cloak belonging to King Stephen I is a sumptuous piece of embroidered silk. The upper floors trawl through a thousand years of history, starting with the period of Árpád rule and concluding with the departure of the last Soviets in 1990.

THE BASICS

hnm.hu

✚ E9

✉ VIII, Múzeum körút 14–16

☎ 1 338 2122

🕐 Tue–Sun 10–6

🍴 Café

🚇 Kálvin tér, Astoria

🚌 9, 15; tram: 47, 49

♿ Access via side entrance on Bródy Sándor utca, where there is a lift. Phone in advance for further assistance

💷 Moderate

❓ Audio tours available, as well as guided tours by advance appointment (☎ 1 327 7749)

Nagy Zsinagóga and Zsidó Múzeum

Nagy Zsinagóga (Great Synagogue) (left); detail of one of the domes (right)

THE BASICS

dohany-zsinagoga.hu
jewishtouringhungary.com

✠ D8 and E8

✉ VII, Dohány utca 2

☎ 1 343 0420

🕐 Mar–Apr, Oct Sun–Thu 10–6, Fri 10–4; May–Sep Sun–Thu 10–8, Fri 10–4; Nov–Feb Mon–Thu 10–4, Fri 10–2

🚇 Astoria, Deák tér

🚌 5, 7, 8E, 110, 112, 133E; trolley-bus: 74; tram: 47, 49

♿ Synagogue: good; museum: none

💰 Expensive

❓ Tours available

DID YOU KNOW?

● Renovation in the 1990s was in part funded by a foundation led by the actor Tony Curtis, whose father was a Hungarian Jew.

TIP

● During the Jewish Summer Festival, concerts are held in the synagogue.

The Great Synagogue is the second-largest synagogue in the world (after New York's). It is a beautiful and imaginative piece of architecture, while its adjacent museum tells of the Holocaust in Hungary.

The Great Synagogue It's impossible to miss the massive, twin-towered Great Synagogue standing on the northern side of Dohány utca. It was built for both Orthodox and Reform Jews, and was finished in 1859. The designer was the Austrian architect Ludwig Förster, and he created an eclectic building topped with Moorish onion domes. The interior is heavily gilded and has separate seating for male and female worshipers. Behind the synagogue is a memorial park on the burial place of many Jews who died of disease and starvation when this area of the city was sealed off as a ghetto.

Jewish Museum The Holocaust hit Hungary in March 1944, when the Germans occupied the country and put the Arrow-Cross Party (the Hungarian Nazis) in control. Over 600,000 of Hungary's Jews were killed or moved to concentration camps. The full program of deportation from Budapest began in late 1944. Half the city's Jews died before the capital was liberated. The Jewish Museum is a moving reminder and contains an exhibition devoted to this period with contemporary photographs. There is also a collection of items relating to Jewish festivals.

Szimpla Kert (left); Trabant car serving as a table (right)

Romkocsma

Ruin pubs have revitalized Budapest's old Jewish Quarter and given rise to an alternative arts and entertainment scene. Housed in the courtyards and rooms of abandoned buildings, they have a vibe that's unique to the city.

The story For decades after World War II, the streets in the shadow of the Great Synagogue languished in disrepair. Although still crumbling and ripe for renovation, it's now the city's liveliest quarter, restored by the advent of ruin pubs *(romkocsma)*. The brainchild of four college graduates who transformed a disused factory into an open-air cinema and bar in 2001, Szimpla Kert (Simple Garden) was the first ruin pub and the blueprint for the many that have followed.

Secreted up side streets Hidden behind dilapidated entrances, each ruin pub is unique, linked only by their locations in run-down buildings, mismatched thrift-shop furnishings and the sheer inventiveness of the decor, from surreal to shabby living room. At Szimpla Kert food is limited to the likes of burgers and sandwiches, but drinks are inexpensive and on Sunday mornings the courtyard hosts a quirky farmers' market. Indie films are screened here, and local bands perform. A communist-era Trabant car doubles as a table. The cavernous building is a mix of indoor and outdoor spaces, its many bars and rooms inhabited, like all ruin pubs, by people of all ages and nationalities.

THE BASICS

ruinpubs.com
szimpla.hu
🚇 E8
✉ Szimpla Kert: VII, Kazinczy utca 14
☎ 20 261 8669
🕐 Daily noon–4am
Ⓜ Astoria
🚌 5, 7, 8E, 110, 112, 133E; tram: 47, 49
♿ Limited

TIP

● Most ruin pubs cluster in the VIIth district, but new ones pop up in mansion blocks, factories, on rooftops and in unused outdoor spaces across the city. To discover the latest hotspot, just ask around.

AROUND BELVÁROS TOP 25

Váci utca

TOP 25

Shopping on Váci utca

🔲 D9
🕐 Shops generally open daily 10–6
🍴 Several cafés, bars and restaurants
🚇 Vörösmarty tér, Ferenciek tere
🚌 5, 7, 7E, 8E, 15, 112, 178; tram: 2, 47, 49
🚢 Vigadó tér
♿ Very good

HIGHLIGHTS

● Thonet House (No. 11)
● City Council Chamber (Nos. 62–64), designed by Imre Steindl in 1870
● Fountain with the statue of the Fisher Girl in Kristóf tér
● White cobbles crossing the street and marking the position of the medieval northern gate to the city (demolished at the end of the 18th century)

Váci utca is the city's best-known street, and is the most central of the tourist arteries. Lined with cafés, bars and shops selling clothes, jewelry, glass and books, it usually thrums with people browsing or taking a stroll.

The street Running parallel to the river (but out of sight of it), Váci utca lasts much of the way through the Belváros. In medieval times, this was the full length of the city of Pest. It has been a spot to promenade and shop since the 18th century, and reached the height of its popularity among the fashionable set in the late 1800s and early 1900s. It was at this time that some of the elegant buildings were constructed, including the Thonet House (at No. 11)—designed by Ödön Lechner, the leading member of the Hungarian art nouveau movement. Some of the original character was sacrificed during so-called communist modernization, but the pedestrianized street has enjoyed something of a renaissance in recent years with the appearance of popular international brands and fashion chains.

Top to tail Two of the city's highlights can be found at either end of Váci utca. Facing the southern end, across Vámház körút, is the Great Market Hall (▷ 75). The northern end opens into Vörösmarty tér. A Christmas market (▷ 77) occupies the square in winter, and it is the home of Gerbeaud (▷ 81), the city's most famous coffeehouse.

More to See

BELVÁROSI PLÉBÁNIATEMPLOM

belvarosiplebania.hu

The Inner City Parish Church is wedged into a tight space beside the Elizabeth Bridge. There was once a Roman fort here—a defensive post across the river from the main town of Aquincum (▷ 102). A church was built in the 11th century (and Bishop Gellért laid to rest inside after being murdered by pagans in the aftermath of King Stephen I's death), but the foundations of the present church date to the 12th century. The sanctuary is medieval; there is a Turkish prayer niche inside, evidence that the Ottomans used it as a place of worship during their occupation.

➕ D9 ✉ V, Március 15 tér ☎ 1 318 3108 🕐 Mon–Sat 11–6, Sun 9–10 🚇 Ferenciek tere 🚌 5, 7, 8E, 112, 178; tram: 2 ♿ Good 💷 Moderate

DUNAKORZÓ

The Pest-side Danube promenade is a popular strolling street running from Elizabeth Bridge up to the Chain Bridge, with the tram tracks just below it. Along the way you'll pass the extravagant 19th-century Vigadó theater, which hosted musical greats like Liszt and Wagner. Look out too for the statue of the Little Princess sitting on the railings; it was placed here in 1989 and is a popular subject of tourist photographs, with the palace facing it across the river.

➕ C8 🍴 Restaurant and café 🚇 Vörösmarty tér 🚌 15, 115; tram: 2 ♿ Good

FERENCES TEMPLOM

pestiferences.ofm.hu

The original 13th-century church on this site was destroyed by the Turks in 1526, after which the Franciscans rebuilt it—only for the Turks to appropriate it as a mosque when they returned and occupied the country for the next 150 years. The current version is 18th-century, with ceiling paintings added later by Károly Lotz. One of the pews

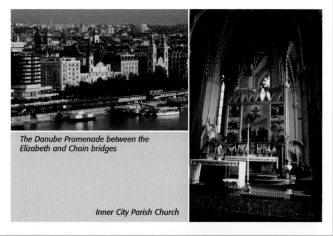

The Danube Promenade between the Elizabeth and Chain bridges

Inner City Parish Church

here was where Franz Liszt used to sit when he stayed in the presbytery in the late 1860s and early 1870s. On the outside of the church is a stone-carved relief of a man pulling citizens into a small rowing boat. This is Miklós Wesselényi, an aristocrat who took to the water during the huge flood that devastated Pest in 1838, and saved a good number of lives by ferrying people away from danger.
🚻 D9 ⊠ V, Ferenciek tere 9 ☎ 1 317 3322 🕐 Daily 6–12, 4–8 🚇 Ferenciek tere 🚌 5, 7, 8, 15, 112, 115, 133E; tram: 2 ♿ Good 💷 Free

FÖLDALATTI VASÚTI MÚZEUM

bkv.hu/en/museums

The diminutive railway museum is housed in a preserved old station (complete with all its original fittings) in the Deák tér underpass. This was the second underground railway line to be built in the world (the first was in London). Keep an eye out for the old train carriages

and the quaint wall tiles made by the Zsolnay factory in Pécs (▷ panel, 78).
🚻 D8 ⊠ Deák tér, underpass ☎ 1 461 6500 🕐 Tue–Sun 10–5 🚇 Deák tér 🚌 9, 15, 16, 105, 115; tram 47, 49 ♿ None 💷 Inexpensive

MAGYAR TERMÉSZETTUDOMÁNYI MÚZEUM

nhmus.hu

The Natural History Museum stands a few kilometers to the southeast of the Belváros along Üllői út. There's an outdoor geological park adjacent to the museum building (displaying rocks in chronological order, the oldest of which dates back a couple of hundred million years), while inside is a two-ton skeleton of a whale (bearing scorch marks from a fire in 1956), an African diorama (featuring a real lake, and stuffed examples of animals including the Nile crocodile and king python), a superb coral-reef

The spire of Ferences templom (left); statue on the church (right)

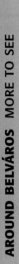

display (spread over 120sq m/
1,291sq ft beneath a glass floor,
and with 200 types of coral, 160
fish and more than 1,000 kinds
of snail, crab and other marine
life) and an exhibition charting
the human use of resources from
the very early period of history
and the impact this has had upon
the natural world. A good rainy day
option with the kids.

🔒 G11 ✉ VIII, Ludovica tér 2–6 ☎ 1 210
1085 🕐 Wed–Mon 10–6 🍽 Café
🚇 Klinikák; Nagyvárad tér 🚊 Tram: 24
♿ Good 💷 Moderate

REFORMÁTUS TEMPLOM

The design of the Calvinist Church
in the busy traffic junction that is
Kálvin tér was begun by József
Hofrichter in 1816 and continued
by József Hild. Its white, neo-
classical exterior has an imposing
portico, while inside the domed
ceiling is barrel vaulted.

🔒 E9 ✉ IX, Kálvin tér 7 ☎ 1 217 6769
🕐 Daily 8–12, 4–6 🚇 Kálvin tér 🚊 9, 15;
tram: 47, 49 ♿ Good 💷 Free

VÁSÁRCSARNOK

piaconline.hu

Constructed at the end of the 19th
century, the Great (or Central)
Market Hall is a Pest institution, an
art-nouveau behemoth facing the
southern opening of Váci utca. It is
most impressive from the outside,
with its patterned roof, while inside
there are stalls spread over three
floors (▷ 78). On the ground and
basement levels you'll find a wide
range of food and drink, including
fresh vegetables, fish and meat,
jars of pickles and caviar, tins of
goose liver and bottles of wine
and fruit brandy. The top floor is
dedicated to craft works and
embroidered lace, and also has
some snack shacks and a buffet
restaurant perfect for a quick beer
after shopping. Throughout the
year there are also themed events
celebrating various world cultures.

🔒 D10 ✉ IX, Vámház körút 1–3 🕐 Mon
6–5, Tue–Fri 6–6, Sat 6–3 🍽 Restaurant
facilities 🚇 Kálvin tér 🚊 15, 115; trolley-
bus: 83; tram: 2, 47, 49 ♿ Good 💷 Free

Great Market Hall

Pest Promenade

This walk covers some choice portions of the heart of the city, including the main square and the river promenade.

DISTANCE: 4km (2.5 miles) **ALLOW:** 1.5–2 hours

START

VÖRÖSMARTY TÉR
🗺 C8 🚇 Vörösmarty tér

1 Begin your walk in Vörösmarty tér, the main square of the Belváros. Prepare with a coffee and cake in the famous Gerbeaud café (▷ 81).

2 Move south from the square along Váci utca (▷ 72), the tourist-thronged shopping street. Look out for the statue of the Fisher Girl in Kristóf tér and the white cobbles marking the medieval northern city gate.

3 At the end of Váci utca's northern stretch, turn left on to Szabadsajtó útja. Walk past the Párisi udvar, popping your head in to admire the highly ornamental decor.

4 Move on to Ferenciek tere with its Franciscan church across the road (▷ 73). Join Kossuth Lajos utca and continue out to the Small Boulevard.

END

ROOSEVELT TÉR
🗺 C8 🚌 15, 16, 105; tram: 2

8 Finish your walk in Roosevelt tér, dominated by the Chain Bridge and the Gresham Palace (▷ 58).

7 Once you reach the Freedom Bridge, join the riverside promenade and head north again. Enjoy the view of the Buda palace, and look out for the Inner City Parish Church (▷ 73) beside Elizabeth Bridge, the Vígadó theater farther up and the statue of the Little Princess on the railings.

6 Cross Kálvin tér, stopping to look at the Calvinist church (▷ 75). Join Vámház körút and follow it back toward the river. Shortly before you reach Freedom Bridge, you'll pass the Great Market Hall (▷ 75) on your left.

5 Turn right on to Múzeum körút. Stop for a turn around the Hungarian National Museum (▷ 68) on the left-hand side of the road.

Shopping

AJKA KRISTÁLY

ajka-crystal.hu

This shop sells Hungary's well-known fine crystal ware, as well as Zsolnay porcelain—perfect options for special souvenirs and gifts.

⊞ D9 ⊠ V, Kossuth Lajos utca 10
☎ 1 328 0844 🕐 Mon–Fri 10–6, Sat 10–1
🚇 Ferenciek tere, Astoria 🚌 7, 8E, 15; tram: 2, 2A

ATTILA SHOES

attilashoes.com

The place to go for bespoke shoes made by a superb craftsman called Attila Kovács. Visit the small shop to have your feet measured, and then choose your preferred style, whether in calf leather or more exotic types like eel and kangaroo. Your shoes will be sent to you a few weeks later.

⊞ D8 ⊠ V, Váci utca 10 ☎ 20 397 6611
🕐 Tue–Sat 10–6 🚇 Vörösmarty tér 🚌 15, 115; tram: 2

BORSZAKÜZLET

malatinszky.hu

One of several outlets run by these producers of premium wine from regions all over Hungary. There are also imported wines on sale (although these are predictable), and there is a useful shipping service.

⊞ C8 ⊠ V, József Attila utca 12 ☎ 20 969 4170 🕐 Mon–Sat 10–6 🚇 Vörösmarty tér
🚌 15, 16, 105

CHRISTMAS MARKET

In December, Vörösmarty tér is filled with around 100 stalls selling quaint Christmas gifts, handcrafted from wood and glass. You can also buy cups of hot mulled wine.

⊞ C8 ⊠ V, Vörösmarty tér 🕐 Throughout Dec 🚇 Vörösmarty tér

FOLKART KÉZMŰVESHÁZ

folkartkezmuveshaz.hu

This is the place to find authentic traditional handicrafts from all the regions of Hungary, including pottery and ceramics, embroidery, linens, lace, felt cushion covers, carpets, carvings, dolls and jewelry. It's a good source of memorable and unique gifts.

⊞ D9 ⊠ V, Regiposta utca 12 ☎ 1 318 5143 🕐 Mon–Fri 10–6, Sat–Sun 10–3 🚌 5, 7, 8E, 15, 115; tram: 2

HERENDI PORCELÁN

herend.com

A shop specializing in pieces of Herend (▷ panel). This fine porcelain has a long and distinguished tradition and is highly regarded for its quality around the world.

⊞ C8 ⊠ V, József nádor tér 11 ☎ 1 317 2622 🕐 Mon–Fri 10–6, Sat 10–2
🚇 Vörösmarty tér 🚌 15, 16, 105, 115

KIRÁLY UTCA

Lined with interior design stores, fashionable boutiques and modern art galleries, Király utca has been dubbed Budapest's design street. At No. 11, the restored Gozsdu Courtyard, formerly the core of the Jewish Quarter, hosts a

HEREND

The village of Herend lies to the north of Lake Balaton (▷ 105). Founded in 1826, the Herend manufactory began making fine, artistic porcelain when it was taken over by Mór Fischer in 1840, and quickly received high acclaim. Among eminent purchasers of Herend pieces were Queen Victoria and Ferenc József I; both have patterns named after them. Today it exports to more than 60 countries and is the world's largest porcelain manufacturer.

ZSOLNAY

The Zsolnay factory in Pécs was established in 1853 by Miklós Zsolnay. His son Vilmos, who took over the company in 1865, experimented with different types of clay and glaze, and devised the unique lustrous finish associated with many Zsolnay pieces. In addition to its ornamental pieces and tableware, Zsolnay gained renown for its so-called pyrogranite ceramic for use on buildings; it is this that is so recognizable in the bright and patterned roofs of buildings like Mátyás Church (▷ 30).

weekly Sunday arts and crafts market from April to October.

🔲 D8 ✉ VII, Király utca 🕐 Shops generally open daily 10–6 🚇 Deák Ferenc tér

PAPRIKA MARKET

paprikamarket.hu

Said to be the city's largest souvenir store, here you can shop for lacework, fruit brandy and of course paprika.

🔲 C8 ✉ V, Vörösmarty tér 1 🕐 Daily 10–6 🚇 Vörösmarty tér 🚌 15, 115; tram: 2

PRÉS HÁZ WINE SHOP AND MUSEUM

preshaz.hu

This wine shop and museum stocks over 300 Hungarian wines from seven regions in the country. It organizes wine-tasting sessions, and showcases traditional items relating to viniculture.

🔲 C8 ✉ V, Váci utca 10 ☎ 1 266 1100 🕐 Mon–Fri 10–7, Sat 10–6 🚇 Vörösmarty tér 🚌 15, 115; tram: 2

SZAMOS MARCIPÁN

szamos.hu

Szamos supplies marzipan to confectioners all over the city. In its small shop just off Váci utca you can buy a range of chocolates and marzipan products, many sculpted into the shape of figurines, flowers or fruits. Good cakes and ice cream are also sold here.

🔲 D9 ✉ V, Párisi utca 3 ☎ 1 317 3643 🕐 Daily 10–7 🚇 Ferenciek tere 🚌 7, 8E, 15, 115

TISZA CIPŐ

tiszacipo.hu

Once a state-owned shoe shop supplying mass-produced sneakers, this store has reinvented itself and now sells clothes as well as shoes. All items are made in Hungary, and the shop is now extremely popular with younger buyers.

🔲 D8 ✉ VII, Károly körút 1 ☎ 1 266 3055 🕐 Mon–Fri 10–7, Sat 10–4 🚇 Astoria 🚌 7, 9, 109; trolley-bus: 74; tram: 47, 49

VÁSÁRCSARNOK

piaconline.hu

Perhaps the city's most famous and vibrant place to shop, this huge indoor market hall has a bustling atmosphere and wares ranging from fresh food and wine to glass and embroidered lace.

🔲 D10 ✉ IX, Vámház körút 1–3 🕐 Mon 6–3, Tue–Fri 6–6, Sat 6–2 (closed Sun, national hols) 🚌 15, 115; trolley-bus: 83; tram: 2, 47, 49

ZSOLNAY PORCELÁN

zsolnay.hu

An outlet selling the distinctive porcelain produced at the famous factory in Pécs (▷ panel) alongside the handpainted and gilded Herend porcelain (▷ 77). Much admired by the Habsburg dynasty and 19th-century aristocrats, some of Herend's classic designs are still manufactured.

🔲 D9 ✉ V, Váci utca 19–21 ☎ 20 330 7053 🕐 Mon–Fri 10–7, Sat 10–6 🚇 Vörösmarty tér 🚌 15, 115; tram: 2

Entertainment and Nightlife

ALCATRAZ
alcatraz.hu

This underground music club and restaurant has a prison theme, with parts of the bar divided between cells. Live bands play funk, blues, rock, soul, jazz and dance. Alcatraz also serves bar food; primarily burgers for soaking up the various cocktails and beers on offer.

➕ E8 ✉ VII, Nyár utca 1 ☎ 30 986 2380 🕐 Fri–Sat 6–5 🚇 Blaha Lujza tér 🚊 5, 7; trolley-bus: 74; tram: 4, 6, 28

BUDAPEST PARK
budapestpark.hu

Outdoor summer festivals happen in this vast space near the Palace of Arts (▷ 80), with headline bands on the main stage. There's a large dance floor, a retro garden, an artists' club and a stage for theater performances. Only used in spring and summer, it is a permanent festival venue.

➕ F12 ✉ IX, Soroksari utca 60 ☎ 1 434 7800 🕐 Apr–Sep daily 5pm–dawn 🚊 23, 54, 55, 103, 179; tram: 1, 2, 24, 51

FAT MO'S
fatmo.hu

Popular with American ex-pats, Fat Mo's is a cellar bar that takes for its theme the era of prohibition in America. Grills, fajitas and pasta are on the menu, and there's live music from 9pm.

➕ D9 ✉ V, Nyáry Pál utca 11 ☎ 1 266 8027 🕐 Sun–Thu 11am–1am, Fri–Sat 11am–2am 🚇 Ferenciek tere 🚊 5, 7, 8, 15, 115, 173, 178; tram: 2

FOGASHÁZ
fogashaz.hu

A ruin pub (▷ 71) in an abandoned building that once housed a dental practice, Fogasház (House of Teeth) and its courtyard garden fuse cultural space and pub. Go for film, theater, art, to meet locals and party on the huge dance floor.

➕ E8 ✉ VII, Akácfa utca 49–51 ☎ 1 783 8820 🕐 House: Thu–Sat 9–5, garden: Sun–Thu 2–4, Fri–Sat 2–5 🚇 Opera, Blaha Lujza tér 🚊 73, 76

IRISH CAT
irishcat.hu

There's plenty about this pub that's traditionally Irish (whiskey, ale, music and events) and plenty that isn't (a selection of pizzas, Hungarian dishes, fruit brandy and retro parties).

➕ E9 ✉ V, Múzeum körút 41 ☎ 1 318 1407 🕐 Daily noon–2am 🚇 Kálvin tér 🚊 8, 9, 15, 109, 115; tram: 47, 49

JANIS' PUB
janispub.hu

Another well-established Irish pub named after legendary singer Janis Joplin. There's a good selection of whiskeys and live sport shown.

➕ D9 ✉ V, Királyi Pál utca 8 ☎ 1 613 4341 🕐 Daily 12–12 🚇 Kálvin tér 🚊 8, 9, 15, 109, 115; tram: 47, 49

DANCE HOUSE

During the communist period, the dance-house (*táncház*) movement grew. This stemmed from a wish to galvanize national identity and culture. People trawled the countryside for examples of traditional dance and music, and then hosted events and classes in urban cultural areas in an attempt to prevent them from dying out. Such dance-house events still take place—find more information on tanchaz.hu—while there are also traditional performances at the National Dance Theater (▷ panel, 35) and an annual Táncház Festival and Fair in March.

MŰVÉSZETEK PALOTÁJA

mupa.hu

The riverside Palace of Arts is the city's main concert hub, and has excellent acoustics and seating for around 2,000 people. Performances range from dance, circus acts, classical music to jazz and opera. It also houses the Ludwig Museum of Modern Arts.

🔛 F12 ✉ IX, Komor Marcell utca 1 ☎ 1 555 3300 🕐 Box office: daily 10–6 🚌 15, 54, 103; tram: 1, 2, 24

NEMZETI SZÍNHÁZ

nemzetiszinhaz.hu

Showcasing classic and contemporary plays, the Hungarian National Theater is surrounded by statue-dotted parkland. This modern building launched the city's new Millennium Quarter, which includes the Palace of Arts (▷ above).

🔛 F12 ✉ IX, Bajor Gizi park 1 ☎ 1 476 6868 🕐 Box office: Mon–Fri 10–6, Sat–Sun 2–6 🚌 23, 54; tram: 1, 2, 24

OLD MAN'S BISTRORÁDAY

eom.hu

This small pub has a retro feel, and a DJ playing music every night. The food served spans soups, burgers and pasta.

🔛 E10 ✉ XI Ráday utca 29 ☎ 30 792 6994 🕐 Sun–Wed 11.30–11, Thu–Sat 11.30am–1am 🚇 Kálvin tér 🚌 15, 115; tram: 4, 6; trolly-bus: 83

PARIS, TEXAS

Among the leading bars on Ráday utca, the sepia pictures that cram the walls lend a cosy, old-time charm.

🔛 E10 ✉ IX, Ráday utca 22 ☎ 1 218 0570 🕐 Daily noon–3am 🚇 Kálvin tér 🚌 9, 15, 109, 115; tram: 47, 49

Where to Eat

PRICES
Prices are approximate, based on a 3-course meal for one person.
€€€   over 7,000Ft
€€   4,000–7,000Ft
€   under 4,000Ft

RED PEPPER (€€)

redpepper.hu

Located behind Vörösmarty tér, beside the British Embassy, this restaurant serves traditional Hungarian and international cuisine, and has some vegetarian options alongside its many specialty lamb dishes.

🔛 C8 ✉ V, Harmincad utca 4 ☎ 20 385 2709 🕐 Daily 12–12 🚇 Vörösmarty tér 🚌 15, 115

CENTRAL KÁVÉHÁZ (€€)

centralkavehaz.hu

Restored, updated, but still reliving the glory days of café society (Central's story dates back to 1887 when it was a meeting place of intellectuals), this is a great place for a shopping pitstop (▷ Váci utca 72). Sadly the service isn't always as great as the setting.

🔛 D9 ✉ V, Károlyi Mihály utca 9 ☎ 1 266 2110 🕐 Daily 8.30am–11pm 🚇 Ferenciek tere 🚌 7, 8E, 15, 178

COSTES (€€€)

costes.hu

Elegant and sophisticated, Costes was the first restaurant in Hungary to gain a Michelin star. The food is exceptional. A second restaurant can be found at V, Vigyázó Ferenc utca 5.

➕ E9 ✉ IX, Ráday utca 4 ☎ 1 219 0696 🕐 Wed–Sun 6.30pm–midnight 🚇 Kálvin tér

FAKANÁL (€)

fakanaletterem.hu

This self-service brasserie on the top floor of the Great (or Central) Market Hall (▷ 75) has excellent-value Hungarian cuisine and live folk music. A great choice for an easy lunch.

➕ D9 ✉ IX, Vámház körút 1–3 ☎ 1 217 7860 🕐 Mon–Fri 9–5, Sat 9–2 🚊 15, 115; trolley-bus: 83; tram: 2, 47, 49

FATÁL (€€)

fatalrestaurant.com

Just off Váci utca (▷ 72), the Fatál— meaning wooden plate—is a busy cellar restaurant serving hearty traditional fare. Given the size of the portions, this place offers great value.

➕ D9 ✉ V, Váci utca 67 ☎ 1 266 2607 🕐 Daily 12–12 🚊 15; tram: 2, 47, 49

GERBEAUD

The super-elegant Gerbeaud (gerbeaud. hu) is the best-known café in Budapest. The owner after which it is named—Emil Gerbeaud—was a late-19th-century Swiss pâtissier who attracted people from miles around to sample his sweet creations. Be sure to try one of the house specials such as the Esterházy or Dobos cakes (▷ panel) and take home treats from the tempting gift shop.

➕ C8 ✉ V, Vörösmarty tér 7–8 ☎ 429 9000 🕐 Daily 9–9 🚇 Vörösmarty tér 🚊 15, 16, 115; tram: 2

DOBOS CAKE

The Dobos cake is lauded by confectioners worldwide. It was the creation of Hungarian pâtissier József Dobos in 1884, and Emperor Ferenc József and his wife were among the first to taste it. The cake consists of five layers of vanilla or lemon sponge spread with chocolate buttercream and topped with caramel, its sides coated with ground nuts. It was unusual both in its simplicity and its use of buttercream (rather than the more familiar whipped cream), and was an immediate hit in Europe.

KÁRPÁTIA (€€€)

karpatia.hu

The Kárpátia can justly stake a claim to being the most beautiful restaurant in the city. Occupying part of the former presbytery of the adjacent Franciscan church, its walls are smothered with historical paintings dating to the 1920s. There is good-quality folk music each evening, and you can choose from the brasserie at the front or the main restaurant. However, the traditional Hungarian food can be patchy.

➕ D9 ✉ V, Ferenciek tere 7–8 ☎ 1 317 3596 🕐 Mon–Sat 11–11, Sun 5–8pm 🚇 Ferenciek tere 🚊 7, 8E, 15, 178

MÁTYÁS PINCE (€€€)

matyaspince.hu

This enormous cellar restaurant serving traditional and contemporary Hungarian cuisine has a Renaissance theme. Its size makes it popular with coach parties. Folk musicians play every night from 7pm and during weekend lunch. There are dance and operetta performances on Wednesdays and Thurdays.

➕ D9 ✉ V, Március 15 tér 7–8 ☎ 1 266 8008 🕐 Daily 11am–midnight 🚇 Ferenciek tere 🚊 5, 7, 8E, 15, 178; tram: 2

MÚZEUM (€€€)

muzeumkavehaz.hu

The Múzeum—named after the Hungarian National Museum next door—is a classy and imposing café and restaurant that has been open since 1885. Its ceiling mural is by the master historicist artist Károly Lotz and the wall tiles are Zsolnay (▷ panel, 78). The food is mainly traditional.

🔢 E9 ✉ VIII, Múzeum körút 12 ☎ 1 267 0375 🕐 Mon–Sat 12–3, 6–12 🚇 Kálvin tér 🚌 8E, 9, 15, 109, 115; tram: 47, 49

NEW YORK KÁVÉHÁZ (€€€)

newyorkcafe.hu

Once a famed literary coffeehouse, after a massive program of refurbishment it reopened as part of the Boscolo Hotel. Worth a visit for the belle epoque opulence.

🔢 F8 ✉ VII, Erzsébet körút 9–11 ☎ 1 886 6167 🕐 Daily 8am–midnight 🚇 Blaha Lujza tér 🚌 5, 7, 178; trolley-bus: 74; tram: 4, 6, 24

ONYX (€€€)

onyxrestaurant.hu

Budapest's second Michelin-starred restaurant, Onyz presents exquisite dishes. For gourmet tastes on a lower budget, go for the four-course set lunch. Reservations are essential and the setting is ultra-stylish so dress up.

🔢 C8 ✉ V, Vörösmarty tér 7–8, entrance on Harmincad utca ☎ 30 508 0622 🕐 Thu–Sat 12–3 (last arrival 1pm), Tue–Sat 6.30–11 (last arrival 8.30). Closed for a week in Jan and 3 weeks in Aug 🚇 Vörösmarty tér/ Deák tér 🚌 7; tram: 2

PARIS BUDAPEST (€€€)

parisbudapest.hu

In the Sofitel Budapest Chain Bridge hotel, with its great river views, this restaurant boasting a show kitchen blends French cuisine and Hungarian flavors with a fine wine list.

🔢 C8 ✉ V, Széchenyi István tér 2 ☎ 1 235 5600/797 🕐 Daily 11–11 🚇 Vörösmarty tér 🚌 16, 105

SPINOZA CAFÉ (€€)

spinozahaz.hu

Located in the Jewish district, the Spinoza—named after the 17th-century Dutch philosopher—is a café and restaurant that harks back to the atmosphere of turn-of-the-20th-century Holland. The food is international. There is also a theatre showing English-language plays.

🔢 D8 ✉ VII, Dob utca 15 ☎ 1 413 7488 🕐 Daily 8–11 🚇 Astoria 🚌 7, 9, 109; trolley-bus: 74; tram: 47, 49

SPOON–THE BOAT (€€€)

spooncafe.hu

The Spoon is located aboard a permanently moored boat on the Pest side of the river near the intercontinental Hotel, and offers a romantic setting with beautiful views. There is a wide selection of international dishes, including a good vegetarian range.

🔢 C8 ✉ V, on the Danube near the Chain Bridge (outside the Intercontinental Hotel) ☎ 1 411 0933 🕐 Daily 12–12 🚌 15, 16, 105, 115; tram: 2

TRATTORIA TOSCANA (€€)

toscana.hu

This riverside Italian restaurant serves both main meals and snacks (such as bruschetta and pizza) prepared in an open kitchen. It is located on the riverside, in between the Erzsébet and Szabadság bridges, so the views from the summer terrace are terrific.

🔢 D9 ✉ V, Belgrád rakpart 13–15 ☎ 1 327 0045 🕐 Daily 12–12 🚌 15, 115; tram: 2

Andrássy út continues northeast from the Great Boulevard, finally opening into the broad Heroes' Square. Beyond is the city's main park, which contains the Széchenyi Baths, as well as a fairy-tale castle and a zoo with an art nouveau elephant house.

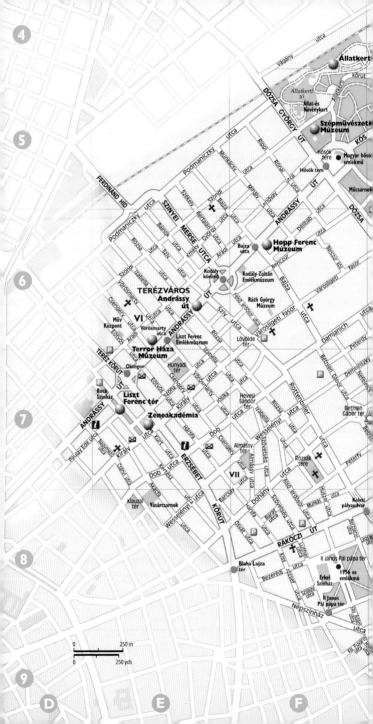

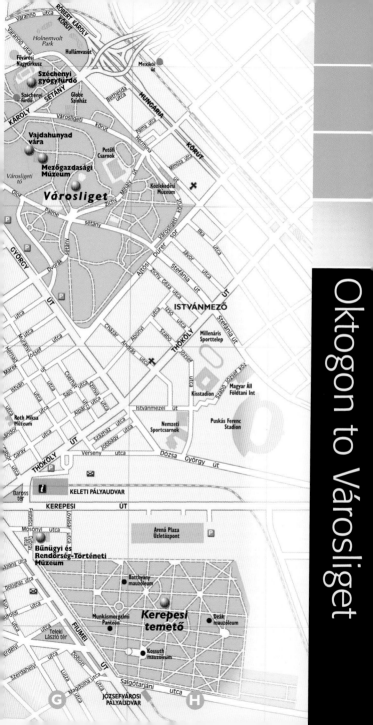

Varannó utca
RÓBERT KÁROLY KÖRÚT
Varannó utca

Holnemvolt Park

Hullámvasút

Mexikói út

HUNGÁRIA

Fővárosi Nagycirkusz

Széchenyi gyógyfürdő

Széchenyi fürdő

SÉTÁNY

Globe Színház

Bethesda utca

Pálma utca

KÁROLY

Városligeti Körút

Hermina

KÖRÚT

Vajdahunyad vára

Petőfi Csarnok

Mimóza utca

Mezőgazdasági Múzeum

Zichy Mihály út

Közlekedési Múzeum

Városligeti tó

Városliget

Palme

setány

Olof

Kárpát

Dvořák

P

Áfonya

Városligeti sor

Ilka utca

Ajtósi Dürer sor

Stefánia út

GYÖRGY

ÚT

zichy Géza utca

Jávor utca

ÚT

P

ISTVÁNMEZŐ

utca

Stefánia út

Chazár András

Abonyi utca

Szabó

THÖKÖLY

Millenáris Sporttelep

utca

Murányi utca

Hernád József utca

Marek

Csanád utca

Szinva utca

Alpár utca

József

Kisstadion

Szabó József köz

Magyar Áll Földtani Int

István

Saj

Roth Miksa Múzeum

Sándor

Garay

Színház utca

Istvánmezei út

Puskás Ferenc Stadion

ÚT

Jobbágy utca

Nemzeti Sportcsarnok

THÖKÖLY

Verseny utca

Dózsa György út

P

Baross tér

✉

ℹ KELETI PÁLYAUDVAR

KEREPESI ÚT

Mosonyi utca

Lovász utca

Festetics György utca

Arená Plaza Üzletközpont

P

Bűnügyi és Rendőrség-Történeti Múzeum

láng utca

Batthyány mauzóleum

Dologház utca

Alföldi utca

Munkásmozgalmi Panteón

Kerepesi temető

Deák mauzóleum

Erdélyi utca

Teleki László tér

FIUMEI

Kossuth mauzóleum

Szerdahelyi utca

Dobozi utca

Magdolna utca

Salgótarjáni utca

ÚT

G

JÓZSEFVÁROSI PÁLYAUDVAR

H

HIGHLIGHTS

● Elegant villas and imposing town houses
● The State Opera House (▷ 52)
● The Lotz terem in the art-nouveau Paris Department Store (▷ 59)
● Liszt Ferenc tér—its terrace cafés are favored meeting places on warm summer nights (▷ 93)
● Millennium Monument on Heroes' Square
● The Museum of Fine Arts (▷ 88–89)—one of Central Europe's leading art collections

TIPS

● Heroes' Square is at its most atmospheric at night, when the column is illuminated.
● Colorful lights and decorations turn Andrássy út into a glittering parade at Christmas.

Arrow-straight, Budapest's most elegant boulevard runs for about 3km (2 miles) from the Small Boulevard up to Hősök tere (Heroes' Square) and Városliget (City Park, ▷ 91).

The history Count Gyula Andrássy's dream of giving the capital a street to rival the Champs Élysées in Paris eventually came to fruition when construction began in 1872. During the Communist period the avenue was known first as Sztálin út and then Népköztársaság (Avenue of the People's Republic). It became Andrássy út once more after the political change in 1990. Since then it has been made a UNESCO World Heritage Site. Trees and elegant architecture, shops, museums, theaters and cafés line the wide avenue, and busy squares punctuate it, as it makes its way to the grand Hősök tere.

Clockwise from left: The colonnades display statues of Hungarian leaders and heroes; an imposing facade on Andrássy út; statue of Jókai

Heroes' Square Created as part of the millennial celebrations in 1896, Hősök tere is the monumental gateway to City Park. It has traditionally been used as the ceremonial stage for state occasions. Two semicircular colonnades with carved figures of Hungary's leaders flank the 36m (118ft) high column that dominates the square. Its plinth is adorned with reliefs of the Magyar tribes who settled in the Carpathian Basin in AD896, the ancestors of today's Hungarians. A tomb dedicated to the victims of the 1956 revolution stands in front of the column.

Fine art Two neoclassical buildings face each other across this vast square, the Museum of Fine Arts (▷ 88–89) and the Hall of Arts (Műcsarnok), which hosts temporary collections and exhibitions.

THE BASICS

- E6 and F5
- Shops generally Mon–Sat 10–7
- Numerous restaurants, bars, cafés
- M1 metro line runs the entire length of the street (between Bajcsy-Zsilinszky út and Hősök tere)
- 105; trolley-bus: 70, 73, 76, 78; tram: 4, 6
- Very good

Szépművészeti Múzeum

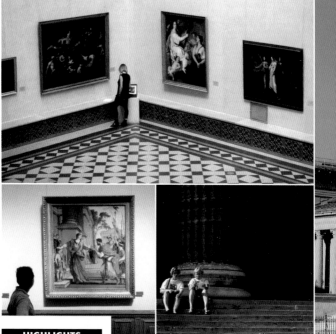

The Museum of Fine Arts—housed in a building looking like a Greek temple—boasts the country's best collection of art from around the world. Its permanent exhibitions are internationally significant.

Egyptian art The museum's collection of Egyptian art is based on finds made during Hungarian archaeological digs in the 20th century. Among the works are mummies and decorated sarcophagi, the carved figure of Prince Sheshong dating to the 9th century BC, and an ivory magic wand fashioned from the tusk of a hippo around 4,000 years ago.

Classical art This collection focuses upon Mediterranean antiquities, and includes Greek, Etruscan, Roman and Graeco-Egyptian art.

Clockwise from left: Gallery in the Museum of Fine Arts; the impressive building is on Heroes' Square; resting on the steps outside the museum; a European painting

Among the exhibits are vases, marble statuettes and items made from glass and bronze. Look out for the Budapest Dancer (a female figure sculpted in ancient Greece), the bronze Grimani Jug and the statues of leading contemporary Romans.

Old Masters The museum's main attraction is its collection of paintings by renowned masters, the bulk acquired from the Eszterházy family in the late 19th century. Many of the greats are represented: there are works by Renaissance artists like Raphael and Titian, Dutch works by Pieter Bruegel the Elder, globally important Spanish paintings featuring El Greco and Goya, and British pieces by Reynolds and Constable. During renovations the 50 most famous works are on display in the Hungarian National Gallery.

THE BASICS

szepmuveszeti.hu
+ F5
⊠ XIV, Dózsa György
út 41
☎ 1 469 7100
🕐 Closed for renovation
until March 2018
🍴 Café
Ⓜ Hősök tere
🚌 20E, 30, 105; trolley-
bus: 72, 75, 79
♿ Very good
💰 Moderate to expensive
❓ Audio guides and
smartphone apps available

89

Terror Háza Múzeum

TOP 25

The chilling House of Terror holds a moving museum

THE BASICS

terrorhaza.hu

➕ E6

✉ VI, Andrássy út 60

☎ 1 374 2600

🕐 Tue–Sun 10–6

Ⓜ Vörösmarty utca, Oktogon

🚌 105; trolley-bus: 73, 76; tram: 4, 6

♿ Good

💰 Moderate

HIGHLIGHTS

● The Soviet tank filling the central courtyard
● Reconstructions of the harrowing prison and torture cells in the basement
● Wall comprising moving photographs of some of the victims of the terror regimes

The House of Terror is a museum that charts the brutal methods employed by the two regimes that terrorized Hungary during the 20th century, and preserves the memory of their many victims.

History The building on Andrássy út is notorious as the place where first the Hungarian Nazis and later the communist secret police incarcerated, tortured and often murdered their victims. From 1940, the fascist Arrow-Cross Party rented it as their headquarters and named the place the House of Faith. After they were installed in government by the Germans in 1944, they used the former coal cellars to hold their primarily Jewish prisoners, many of whom died here. After the "liberation" of Budapest by the Soviets in January 1945, the communist political police (including the much-feared ÁVÓ) took over the building, deliberately cultivating its reputation as the "House of Horror." They joined the cellars together, creating a maze of cells in which to imprison, torture and interrogate political opponents. Before the building was overrun by revolutionaries in 1956, the secret police meticulously cleared evidence of their activities.

The exhibition Deliberately innovative and evocative, the museum's daring approach divides opinion. There is video footage and photographs, together with police uniforms, the testimony of former prisoners and reconstructed torture cells.

Városliget

City Park lies behind Heroes' Square and is the capital's main piece of parkland. A haven in summer and winter alike, it has a zoo, circus, massive spa complex and a romantic castle.

The history The rectangular City Park was once the venue for markets and Diets (legislative assemblies). It was transformed into a recreational park at the beginning of the 19th century, and was a space used equally by workers who hosted meetings here and nobles who took turns around it in their carriages and finery. Its greatest hour came in 1896, when it was the focal point for the millennial celebrations and held a great exhibition of Hungarian products, inventions and achievements.

The park today The park's main feature is its artificial lake, which is used for boating during the summer and is frozen in winter to serve as an outdoor ice rink. A bridge leads over this from the rear of Heroes' Square, and a series of paths run across the park's grass and around its trees. The northwestern section of the park contains a zoo (▷ 92), a circus that also hosts shows and Gundel, Budapest's most famous restaurant. Here too are the Széchenyi Baths (▷ 93), the largest complex in Central Europe, where you can take an soak at any time of the year. The intriguing Vajdahunyad Castle (▷ 94) stands on an island in the middle of the lake. Look out for the statue of the 12th-century chronicler, Anonymus, on the main walkway.

THE BASICS

➕ G5

🍴 Robinson restaurant and café, Gundel restaurant, Bagolyvár restaurant (▷ 98)

🚇 Széchenyi fürdő; Hősök tere

🚌 20E, 30, 105; trolley-bus: 72, 74, 75, 79; tram: 1

♿ Good

HIGHLIGHTS

● Széchenyi Baths (▷ 93)
● The lake
● Állatkert (zoo, ▷ 92)
● Vajdahunyad Castle (▷ 94), containing the Museum of Agriculture (▷ 93)

TIP

● During the summer months there are frequent classical and modern concerts performed on a stage in the lake with the castle as a backdrop.

More to See

ÁLLATKERT

zoobudapest.com

Budapest Zoo opened 150 years ago, and has striking art-nouveau buildings dating from the early 1900s—be sure to visit the Moorish elephant house. The zoo holds more than 2,000 species of animal, and has enclosures dedicated to the African savannah and the Arctic. There's a daily program of events.

🔛 F4 ⊠ XIV, Állatkerti körút 6–12 ☎ 1 273 4902 🕐 Mar, Oct Mon–Thu 9–5, Fri–Sun 9–5.30; Apr, Sep Mon–Thu 9–5.30, Fri–Sun 9–6; May–Aug Mon–Thu 9–6, Fri–Sun 9–7; Nov–Feb daily 9–4 🍴 Café 🚇 Széchenyi fürdő 🚌 20E, 30, 105; trolley-bus: 72, 75, 79 🚹 Very good 🎫 Expensive

BŰNÜGYI ÉS RENDŐRSÉG-TÖRTÉNETI MÚZEUM

rendormuzeum.com

The Museum of Crime and Police History charts the development of law enforcement in Hungary. Among the exhibits are former uniforms, firearms and medals dating from 1848 to the present day, as well as rather gory details of famous murder cases.

🔛 G8 ⊠ VIII, Mosonyi utca 5 ☎ 1 477 2183 🕐 Tue–Sat 9–5 🚇 Keleti pályaudvar 🚌 5, 7, 20E, 30, 178; trolley-bus: 73, 76; tram: 24 🚹 Good 🎫 Free

HOPP FERENC MÚZEUM

hoppmuseum.hu

Ferenc Hopp was a keen collector of Oriental art, and when he died in 1919 he donated his collection of over 4,000 works to the state. Today his villa on Andrássy út hosts exhibitions focused on Asian art and culture.

🔛 F6 ⊠ I, Andrássy út 103 ☎ 1 469 7759 🕐 Tue–Sun 10–6 🚇 Bajza utca 🚌 105 🚹 Good 🎫 Moderate

KEREPESI TEMETŐ

norigov.hu

Spreading across almost 55ha (136 acres), the National Cemetery is a tranquil spot. Paths lined with chestnut trees lead past rows of graves and mausoleums,

The elephant house at Budapest Zoo

Kerepesi Cemetery

many of them holding Hungary's historical greats. Among a number of impressive marble mausoleums are those of Ferenc Deák and Lajos Kossuth.

🔲 H8 ☒ VIII, Fiumei út 16 ☎ 70 400 8362 🕓 Nov–Feb 7.30–5, Mar 7–5.30, Sep 7–6, Apr–Aug 7–7, May–Jul 7–8 🚇 Keleti pályaudvar 🚌 99, 217E; trolley-bus: 80; tram: 24, 28, 37 🅰 Few 🎫 Free

LISZT FERENC TÉR

Named after the Hungarian composer, Franz Liszt, this is one of the leading spots for socializing in the city, a long square lined on each side with café-bars and restaurants. It gets busy in summer, when everyone enjoys the sunshine sat at tables outside. Indeed, even in winter there are customers who choose to drink outside beneath the gas heaters and blankets that many of the bars provide.

🔲 E7 ☒ VI, Liszt Ferenc tér 🕓 Bars and restaurants generally open noon–2am 🚇 Oktogon 🚌 105; trolley-bus: 70, 78; tram: 4, 6 🅰 Good

MEZŐGAZDASÁGI MÚZEUM

mezogazdasagimuzeum.hu

The Museum of Agriculture is the largest of its type in Europe, with 12 permanent exhibitions, and occupies the main wing of the Vajdahunyad Castle (▷ 94). Among the subjects covered by the display are Hungarian livestock breeding, the lives of shepherds on the Great Plain, and the history of viniculture, hunting and fishing (including a prehistoric canoe found at Lake Balaton, ▷ 105).

🔲 G5 ☒ XIV, Városliget ☎ 1 422 6765 🕓 Apr–Oct Tue–Sun 10–5; Nov–Mar Tue–Fri 10–4, Sat–Sun 10–5 🍴 Café 🚇 Széchenyi fürdő 🚌 20, 30, 105; tram: 1; trolley-bus: 70, 72, 74, 75, 79 🅰 Good 🎫 Moderate

SZÉCHENYI GYÓGYFÜRDŐ

szechenyibath.hu

The huge, neo-baroque building near the zoo in City Park holds the Széchenyi Baths, one of the biggest spas in Europe. The architecture is impressive, and

Zeneakadémia (Ferenc Liszt Academy of Music)

Széchenyi Baths

among the many pools (there are 21 to choose from) is a large outdoor bath.

🚩 G5 ✉ XIV, Állatkerti körút 9–11 ☎ 1 363 3210 🕓 Daily 6am–10pm 🍴 Café 🚇 Széchenyi fürdő 🚌 Trolley-bus: 72 ♿ Good 💷 Expensive

VAJDAHUNYAD VÁRA

vajdahunyadcastle.com

One of the most intriguing buildings you're likely to come across, Vajdahunyad Castle was made from wood as a show piece for the Millennial Exhibition in 1896. It was so popular that it was rebuilt in stone afterwards. Its designer, Ignác Alpár, drew upon more than 20 historical architectural styles from around the country. The castle was named after the main part facing across the lake, which was fashioned on the 15th-century Transylvanian family pile of János Hunyadi, the victorious leader of the struggle against the Turks. The Museum of Agriculture (▷ 93) is inside the castle, but it's free to walk around the courtyards to see the palace, the Statue of Anonymus and the Jak Chapel, a Romanesque church where Catholic services are held from spring to autumn at noon.

🚩 G5 ✉ XIV, Városliget ☎ 1 363 1973 🕓 Courtyard open daily 24 hours 🚇 Széchenyi fürdő 🚌 Trolley-bus: 70, 72, 74, 75, 79 ♿ Good 💷 Free

ZENEAKADÉMIA

zeneakademia.hu

The Ferenc Liszt Academy of Music was founded by Liszt in 1875. The fabulous art-nouveau central building on Liszt Ferenc tér dates to 1907. Among those to have taught and studied here are Béla Bartók, Zoltán Kodály, Ernő Dohnányi and Leó Weiner. Recitals and concerts are given in the Grand Hall and Sir Georg Solti Chamber Hall.

🚩 E7 ✉ VI, Liszt Ferenc tér 8 ☎ 1 462 4100 🚇 Oktogon 🚌 105; trolley-bus: 70, 78; tram: 4, 6 ♿ Call in advance on 462 4636 ❓ Daily tours in English at 1.30, expensive

Vajdahunyad Castle

A Walk to the Park

This walk takes in Budapest's most elegant avenue, most imposing square and main park.

DISTANCE: 4km (2.5 miles) **ALLOW:** 2–3 hours

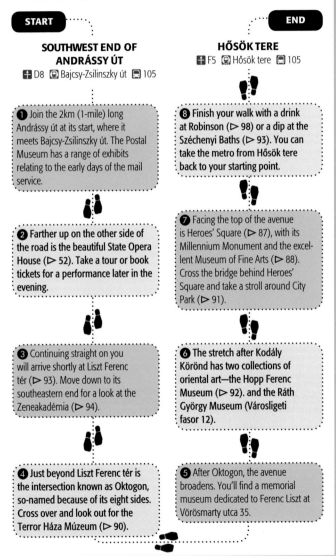

START

SOUTHWEST END OF ANDRÁSSY ÚT

D8 Bajcsy-Zsilinszky út 105

1 Join the 2km (1-mile) long Andrássy út at its start, where it meets Bajcsy-Zsilinszky út. The Postal Museum has a range of exhibits relating to the early days of the mail service.

2 Farther up on the other side of the road is the beautiful State Opera House (▷ 52). Take a tour or book tickets for a performance later in the evening.

3 Continuing straight on you will arrive shortly at Liszt Ferenc tér (▷ 93). Move down to its southeastern end for a look at the Zeneakadémia (▷ 94).

4 Just beyond Liszt Ferenc tér is the intersection known as Oktogon, so-named because of its eight sides. Cross over and look out for the Terror Háza Múzeum (▷ 90).

END

HŐSÖK TERE

F5 Hősök tere 105

8 Finish your walk with a drink at Robinson (▷ 98) or a dip at the Széchenyi Baths (▷ 93). You can take the metro from Hősök tere back to your starting point.

7 Facing the top of the avenue is Heroes' Square (▷ 87), with its Millennium Monument and the excellent Museum of Fine Arts (▷ 88). Cross the bridge behind Heroes' Square and take a stroll around City Park (▷ 91).

6 The stretch after Kodály Körönd has two collections of oriental art—the Hopp Ferenc Museum (▷ 92). and the Ráth György Museum (Városligeti fasor 12).

5 After Oktogon, the avenue broadens. You'll find a memorial museum dedicated to Ferenc Liszt at Vörösmarty utca 35.

Entertainment and Nightlife

DÜRER KERT

durerkert.com

At Dürer Garden, a ruin pub (▷ 71) in a former university building on the southern edge of City Park (▷ 91), you can play table tennis, table football, darts and pétanque, chill out or dance to DJs and live concerts featuring indie, hardcore, electro, gumipop and death-disco, in the garden or outdoors.

➕ H6 ✉ XIV, Ajtósi Dürer sor 19–21 ☎ 1 789 4444 🕐 Daily 5pm–5am 🚍 Trolley-bus: 74, 75; tram: 1

INCOGNITO

The longest-standing bar on Liszt Ferenc tér, Incognito remains a favorite. Choose a cocktail to enjoy from the extensive drinks menu. It has an outside terrace and hosts party events.

➕ E7 ✉ VI, Liszt Ferenc tér 3 ☎ 70 639 0094 🕐 Tue–Thu 4pm–midnight, Fri–Sat 4pm–3am 🚇 Oktogon 🚍 105; trolley-bus: 70, 78

KIADÓ KOCSMA

The Kiadó extends over two levels, with ground-floor and cellar areas. It nods towards the British pub in some of its furnishings, and serves filling food in good-size portions. It's a popular spot with students.

➕ E7 ✉ VI, Jókai tér 3 ☎ 1 331 1955 🕐 Mon–Fri 10am–1am, Sat, Sun 11am–1am 🚇 Oktogon 🚍 105; trolley-bus: 70, 78

PAPP LÁSZLÓ SPORTARÉNA

budapestarena.hu

Named after the Olympic champion boxer, and nicknamed "the pebble", this indoor arena for sports and cultural events hosts concerts by Hungarian and international performers.

➕ J7 ✉ XIV, Stefánia út 2 ☎ 1 422 2600 🚇 Puskas Ferenc Stadion 🚍 130; trolley-bus: 75, 77, 80; tram: 1

PUSKÁS FERENC STADION

The country's main sports stadium is named after the great Hungarian foot-baller of the 1950s. In addition to football matches and athletics events, the outdoor stadium is the venue for big concerts and other shows. The stadium is currently being rebuilt and is due to reopen in 2019.

➕ H7 ✉ XIV, Istvánmezei út 3–5 ☎ 1 471 4100 🚇 Stadionok 🚍 130; trolley-bus: 75, 77; tram: 1

STEFÁNIA PALOTA

bphkk.hu

This old officers' club is now the venue for a cultural center. Inside is a library and a restaurant, and there are regular balls, concerts, exhibitions and a night-club on weekends. The place also offers a variety of programs for children.

➕ H6 ✉ XIV, Stefánia út 34–36 ☎ 1 383 4958 🚍 5, 7, 112; trolley-bus: 72, 74, 75

HELLO BABY BAR & CLUB

A large "ruin pub/club" occupying a former 19th-century mansion near Oktogon. There are five bars, and two dancefloors, often with international DJs.

➕ E7 ✉ VI, Andrássy út 52 ☎ 20 776 0767 🕐 Fri–Sat 10pm–5am 💵 2,000Ft (of which 1,000Ft redeemable for drinks) 🚇 Metro: Oktogon 🚍 105; Tram: 4, 6

COMMUNIST REMINDERS

When the Népstadion—which means "People's Stadium"—was first erected in 1953, the avenue leading up to it was lined with statues of sport and endeavor in the socialist-realist style. Around 16 of these survive today and can be viewed in the garden of the Puskás Ferenc Stadion (the stadium's name since 2002). Seating 60,000, it is Hungary's largest stadium.

Where to Eat

BAGOLYVÁR (€€)

bagolyvar.com

"Owl Castle" is cheaper and more relaxed than Gundel next door. The restaurant takes pride in its traditional, home-cooked food and also offers vegetarian and children's menus.

➕ F5 ✉ XIV, Gundel Károly út 4 ☎ 1 889 8127 🕐 Daily 12–12 🚇 Hősök tere 🚌 30, 105; trolley-bus: 72, 75, 79

GUNDEL (€€€)

gundel.hu

Gundel is Budapest's most famous restaurant, and until fairly recently its status as the city's best stood largely unchallenged. There has been a restaurant here since 1894, but it was after the Gundel family took over in 1910 and gave it their name that it began to receive international acclaim. It oozes old-fashioned elegance and you should dress smartly. As well as the à-la-carte options, the menu also has several fixed-price banquets. The restaurant's signature dish is the Gundel *palacsinta*, a pancake with walnuts and chocolate sauce. On Sunday there's a cheaper all-you-can-eat brunch.

➕ F5 ✉ XIV, Gundel Károly út 4 ☎ 1 889 8111 🕐 Daily 12–12, Sun brunch 11.30–3 🚇 Hősök tere 🚌 105; trolley-bus: 72, 75, 79

INDIGO (€€)

indigo-restaurant.hu

This Indian restaurant serves good food, including a wide range of vegetarian options and delicious tandoor dishes all at reasonable prices. The chefs specialize in mughlai and north Indian cuisine.

➕ D6 ✉ VI, Jókai utca 13 ☎ 1 428 2187 🕐 Daily 12–11 🚇 Oktogon 🚌 Tram: 4, 6

KLASSZ (€€)

klasszetterem.hu

Owned by the Budapest Wine Society, Klassz serves good food at reasonable prices. You can't book a table but it's worth the wait. It also has a wine shop.

➕ E7 ✉ VI, Andrássy út 41 ☎ No phone reservations 🕐 Daily 11.30–11 🚇 Oktogon 🚌 105; trolley-bus: 70, 78

LA PERLE NOIRE (€€€)

laperlenoire.hu

Serving up top-quality Hungarian and French cuisine by noted chefs in the Mamaison Hotel Andrássy, this is an elegant restaurant with a pretty terrace.

➕ F5 ✉ VI, Andrássy út 111 ☎ 1 462 2189 🕐 Daily 12–12 🚇 Bajza utca 🚌 105

MAGDALENA MERLO (€)

magdalenamerlo.hu

This simple restaurant serves mainly Italian food, although there are also some Hungarian and Czech choices. It's perfect for an inexpensive lunch.

➕ E7 ✉ VII, Király utca 59B ☎ 1 322 3278 🕐 Daily 10am–midnight 🚌 Trolley-bus: 70, 78; tram: 4, 6

ROBINSON (€€€)

robinsonrestaurant.hu

The Robinson has a relaxed and pagoda-like feel to it. The menu features international food with rotisserie-cooked meat a feature of the upper floor.

➕ G5 ✉ XIV, Városligeti tó ☎ 1 422 0222 🕐 Daily 11–11 🚇 Hősök tere/Széchenyi Fürdő 🚌 105; trolley-bus: 72, 75, 79

For those willing to explore beyond the capital, there are some lovely attractions within easy reach and worth considering even if you're only on a short break of three or four days.

Pilis-
csaba

PILISVÖRÖSVÁR

Pilisszentiván

Pilisborosjenő

10

Solymár

Téglagyár

Arany-hegyi-patak

0   5 km
0   3 miles

Nagykovácsi

PESTHIDEGKÚT

Budajenő

Telki

B u d a i -

h e g y s é g

RÓZSADOMB

Páty

BUDAKESZI

M1

BIATORBÁGY

BUDAÖRS

M1

Pecato
üdülőtelep

Ko-er

TÖRÖKBÁLINT

*Memento
Park*

BUDAFOK

M0

Sóskút

M7

Diósd

BUDATÉTÉNY

7

Benta

ÉRDLIGET

M6

Duna

TUSZKULÁNUM

Aquincum

Women dressed in Roman costume at Aquincum (left); a Corinthian capital (right)

THE BASICS

aquincum.hu

➕ See map ▷ 101

✉ III, Szentendrei út 135

☎ 1 250 1650

🕐 Apr–Oct Tue–Sun 10–6; Nov–Mar Tue–Sun 10–4

🚌 34, 106, 134

🚆 Aquincum (HÉV suburban railway)

♿ Grounds: few; museum: none

💷 Moderate

HIGHLIGHTS

● Rare 3rd-century water organ, discovered at the site in the early 1930s
● Small amphitheatre right next to Aquincum railway station
● Mosaics discovered in the governor's palace, some with black-and-white geometric patterns from the 2nd century and others with vibrant scenes dating to the 3rd century

Aquincum, on the Buda side of the river, was the area settled by the Romans and it contains a rich collection of remains from that period. You can see the best of them at the Aquincum Museum.

Ample water The Romans arrived in what is now Budapest in 35BC, using the river as a natural defensive barrier defining the eastern edge of their empire. Celts had occupied this area before them, calling it Ak-Ink—meaning Ample Water—and the Romans adopted a version of the name (Aquincum). The settlement was originally established by civilian workers to provide infrastructure and support for the garrison of soldiers in Óbuda, a short distance to the south. The Romans stayed for nearly four centuries, and over that period the town grew in size and importance until Aquincum eventually became the provincial capital of Pannonia Inferior.

Aquincum Museum The excellent museum has a large archaeological park containing surviving walls and foundations from the town of Aquincum, including a public baths complex, temples and a courthouse. In addition, a neo-classical building in the middle of the park displays some of the many valuable finds made during excavation of the area. The lapidarium holds over 1,000 stone items such as sculpted grave markers and sarcophagi. There is also a collection of mosaics and there are frequent temporary exhibits.

View of Budapest from János-hegy (left); rock climbers descend Palvölgy Cave (right)

Budai-hegység

Behind the Castle District and the other settlements along the river lie the Buda Hills, an area that offers good walking and cycling trails. Buses run into the hills, and there are also a couple of characterful railway lines.

The hills A preferred means of getting into the hills is aboard the Cogwheel Railway. You join this at Városmajor station, to the west of Széll Kálmán tér along Szilágyi Erzsébet fasor. On disembarking at Széchenyi-hegy, you can follow walking trails to the Széchenyi Lookout Tower or to János-hegy, the highest of the hills. Alternatively you can join the Children's Railway, whose line runs through popular spots like Normafa lejtő and János-hegy. All the railway staff (except the driver) are children; this apprentice scheme was set up in 1948 by the communist youth movement. Normafa lejtő has wooden tables and is a good spot for a weekend picnic. János-hegy holds the white-stone Elizabeth Viewing Tower, which offers beautiful views.

Other sights The Budakeszi Game Park, near Szépjuhászné station on the Children's Railway, contains game species as well as ancient domestic breeds. The Béla Bartók Memorial House (II, Csalán út 29) preserves some of the composer's possessions in the villa he lived in before he moved to America. There are Hungarian paintings and other exhibits at the Kiscelli Museum (III, Kiscelli utca 108).

THE BASICS

➕ See map ▷ 100
✉ District XII
🚌 57, 63, 64, 155, 157, 291; tram: 18; Cogwheel Railway; Children's Railway; chairlift

HIGHLIGHTS

● The chairlift running up János-hegy
● The Elizabeth Viewing Tower on János-hegy
● The Cogwheel Railway

Memento Park

TOP
25

A bust among the trees (left); the striding sailor that is the symbol of the park (right)

THE BASICS

mementopark.hu

⊞ See map ▷ 100

✉ XXII, Balatoni út (corner of Szabadkai utca)

☎ 1 424 7500

🕐 Daily 10–dusk

🚌 Special bus from Deák tér at 11 (also at 3 in Jul–Aug), bus 101 and 150 from Kelenföld Vasútállomás (terminal of M4 metro line)

♿ Good

💷 Moderate

❓ Guided tours with advance reservation

HIGHLIGHTS

● Republic of Councils Monument—the famous striding, open-shirted sailor that adorns most of the park's promotional literature

● Béla Kun Memorial

● Marx and Engels statues

● Workers' Movement Memorial—a pair of hands enveloping a red orb

Unlike many other former eastern-bloc countries, Hungary preserved rather than destroyed the statues that once looked over its squares and boulevards. They now stand in Memento Park.

The park Memento Park was opened in 1993 on the second anniversary of the departure of Soviet troops from Hungary. There are 42 works on display, gathered from the city's streets and varying from enormous statues to small reliefs or busts. You'll find tributes to Marx and Engels, as well as one to Lenin that used to stand on the edge of City Park; Stalin, however, is not represented because the only statue of him was destroyed by a crowd during the 1956 Revolution. A statue of a Soviet soldier near the entrance once guarded the base of the Freedom Monument (▷ 46). There is also a memorial to Béla Kun by Imre Varga. Kun was leader of the 1919 communist regime called the Republic of Councils; in revenge for a failed anti-communist coup he executed almost 600 people during what came to be known as the "Red Terror." The Barrack Exhibition includes archive footage of secret police training exercises.

The shop You'll find an intriguing range of fun souvenirs in the shop, including original Soviet medals, models of Trabant cars, recordings of famous songs of the communist movement and a can purporting to contain the "last breath of communism."

Excursions

ESZTERGOM

Standing on the Danube Bend, Esztergom was once the country's most important city. It was the royal capital until the 13th century (when Béla IV made Buda the seat of power), and was where King Stephen was crowned. It remains the center of the Roman Catholic Church in Hungary, and it is appropriate that the basilica is the largest in the country. The cathedral's treasury holds a dazzling array of religious items, the oldest dating back to the time of the Árpáds. Nearby is the Royal Palace, where King Stephen is said to have been born.

THE BASICS

Distance: 50km (31 miles)
Journey Time: 1–1.5 hours by train, coach or hydrofoil (latter May–Sep Tue–Sun), 3.5 hours by standard boat (May–Sep Tue–Sun)
🚌 Coach from Árpád híd
🚆 From Nyugati Station
🚢 From Vigadó tér pier
ℹ️ Mahart Passnave ticket office ☎ 1 484 4000; mahartpassrame.hu

LAKE BALATON

The largest freshwater lake in Central Europe lies southwest of the capital. It measures nearly 80km (50 miles) in length, and is often referred to as the Hungarian sea. Under communism, Lake Balaton's beaches and opportunities for water sports made it the most popular summer-holiday destination for Hungarians, and it remains the leading spot for domestic tourism. Its two sides are very different in character. The southern shore is the place for partying, with the main town of Siófok well served with nightclubs, restaurants and resort hotels. The northern shore is prettier and more cultured: Keszthely is a university town with a castle, Tihany has quaint fishermen's cottages and a medieval abbey church, and the plateau of Badacsony is a wonderful backdrop to wine-tasting sessions.

THE BASICS

Distance: 89km (55 miles)
Journey Time: 1.5 hours by train, 2 hours by coach
🚌 Coach from Népliget
🚆 From Déli Station
ℹ️ Víztorony (water tower), Siófok ☎ 84 310 117

THE BASICS

Distance: 19km (12 miles)
Journey Time: 40 mins by HÉV, 1.5 hours by boat, 30 mins by coach
🚌 Coach from Árpád híd
🚊 HÉV from Batthyány tér
⛴ From Vigadó tér pier
ℹ Dumtsa Jenő utca 22
☎ (26) 317 965

SZENTENDRE

Szentendre (meaning St. Andrew) is probably the prime excursion point for tourists venturing beyond the capital; the most enjoyable way to reach it is on the ferry, although it's a short drive or trip aboard the HÉV suburban railway. In the early 20th century, there was an artists' colony here and painters still draw inspiration from its river views and cobbled streets. The town has a good number of museums and galleries, including a Marzipan Museum and an exceptional Open-Air Ethnographic Museum that showcases traditional architecture from regions all over the country. To the south of the town are the remains of a Roman military camp.

THE BASICS

Distance: 30km (19 miles)
Journey Time: 1 hour by train, 1.5 hours by coach, 3.5 hours by boat
🚌 Coach from Árpád híd
🚊 From Nyugati Station
⛴ From Vigadó tér pier
ℹ Rév utca 15
☎ (26) 398 160

VISEGRÁD

Farther around the Danube Bend is Visegrád, a historical town built in a position that affords stunning views of the river. In the 14th century, this town became the royal seat under King Károly Robert. Subsequent kings enlarged and improved upon the royal palace; a visitor during the reign of King Mátyás described it as "paradise on earth." Over the years, however, its faded stonework became buried and some even questioned the existence of the legendary palace. However, the site was finally uncovered in the early 20th century, and it has since been reconstructed. There is now a museum inside relating its history. Nearby is Solomon's Tower and above that the citadel.

HOTEL GELLÉRT GYÓGY

Budapest has accommodation to suit all tastes and pockets. You can choose to stay in a luxury spa hotel, a historic hotel dating to the late 19th century, a hostel dormitory or a family-run bed and breakfast in the Buda Hills.

Introduction

Budapest's popularity as a tourist and conference destination has given rise to many good-quality hotels and luxury international brands with excellent facilities.

Where to Stay

You'll find hotels in most quarters of the city, but tourists usually restrict their search to four or five spots. The Belváros and just beyond—with the bars, restaurants and shops—contain many of the luxury hotels. Most of the city's historic hotels have been upgraded to international standards. There are generally cheaper hotels near City Park, which has several attractions and is within easy reach of Liszt Ferenc tér and the heart of the city. A few hotels make use of the river views on both the Buda and Pest sides. The best-value and most vibrant of the pensions (bed-and-breakfast guesthouses) dot the Buda Hills, and are perfect for those who wish to escape the crowds.

What to Expect

Apart from in hostels, you can usually expect your room to have at least a television and en-suite bathroom, but there are also a few places offering apartment-style rooms which can come with kitchen facilities. There is little inexpensive accommodation in the middle of the city—a place calling itself a pension *(panzió)* in Pest will often be more like a mid-range hotel. Budget visitors should check out hostels, or consider booking a private or college room (the latter offered during vacation periods). Booking agencies can sort these out for you.

SAVING MONEY

Hotels are at their most expensive in high season (between May and October and at Christmas/New Year) and during festivals or major events. However, weekend-break discounts are common, and many hotels participate in a winter promotion offering four nights for the price of three. Rates will usually drop for stays of several days or for advance reservations. Always check the hotel's own website for specials.

Budget Hotels

ADINA APARTMENT HOTEL

tfehotels.com/adina

The Adina is superb value, with facilities —including a swimming pool, fitness room and sauna—coming at a surprisingly reasonable price. Its apartments are spacious, and have fully equipped kitchenettes. Most have balconies. The hotel sits north of the Small Boulevard, around a 15-minute walk to the centre.

🔲 D4 ✉ XIII, Hegedűs Gyula utca 52 ☎ 1 236 8888 🚇 Lehel tér 🚌 15, 115; trolley bus: 76

BRODY 16

brodyhousegroup.com

14 creatively decorated apartments, filled with homemade furniture and local artworks. Apartments have small kitchens and some even have washing machines.

🔲 D7 ✉ VI, Paulay Ede utca 16 ☎ 1 266 1211 🚇 Opera or Bajcsy-Zsilinszky út; 🚌 105

CSÁSZÁR HOTEL

csaszarhotel.hu

Located near Margaret Bridge, this mid-size hotel shares a building with the Komjádi-Császár swimming pool. Each room has a bathroom, TV and minibar.

🔲 B4 ✉ II, Frankel Leó utca 35 ☎ 1 336 2640 🚌 9, 17; tram: 4, 6, 17

GÓLIÁT HOTEL

gerandhotels.hu

This mid-size hotel stands near City Park (▷ 91). The rooms have a toilet, but showers are on the corridors.

🔲 G3 ✉ XIII, Kerekes utca 12–20 ☎ 1 350 1456 🚌 30, 32, 105; tram: 1

KALMÁR PENSION

pensionkalmar.com

This 10-room guesthouse near the Gellért Baths is as quirky and characterful as they come, and very possibly the best-value accommodation in the city. The building was first constructed for Count Pál Teleki, an early-20th-century prime minister of Hungary, and the interior retains a historical feel, with antique furniture and oil paintings. Some rooms even have kitchenettes.

🔲 C10 ✉ XI, Kelenhegyi út 7–9 ☎ 30 271 9312 🚇 Szent Gellért tér 🚌 7, 133E; tram: 41, 47, 48, 49, 56

MAGAZINE HOTEL

themagazinehotel.com

Magazine Hotel has a fantastic position in an elegant residential building on St. Stephen's Square, and some of its rooms even overlook the Basilica itself. There are 12 rooms and four apartments, all with parquet flooring and simple, yet strikingly stylish, furnishings. Among the facilities are a small dining area and a kitchen.

🔲 D7 ✉ V, Szent István tér 4 ☎ 70 611 1088 🚇 Deák tér or Bajcsy-Zsilinszky út 🚌 16, 105

Mid-Range Hotels

ART'OTEL
artotels.com
A fashionable design hotel in Buda, across from the Parliament building (▷ 54), featuring original works by American contemporary artist Donald Sultan (there are daily art tours).
🚇 B7 ✉ I, Bem Rakpart 16–19 ☎ 1 487 9487 🚇 Batthyány tér 🚊 Tram: 19, 41

ASTORIA
danubiushotels.com
The Astoria is based in a graceful turn-of-the-20th-century building on the Small Boulevard and has an atmospheric café-restaurant.
🚇 D9 ✉ V, Kossuth Lajos utca 19–21 ☎ 1 889 6000 🚇 Astoria 🚊 7, 109, 178; tram: 47, 49

BALTAZÁR
baltazarbudapest.com
A boho-chic boutique hotel with heaps of personality in the Castle District. Each room has a unique and creative design, and the restaurant is top drawer.
🚇 A7 ✉ I, Országház utca 31 ☎ 1 300 7050 🚊 16, 16A, 116

BUDA CASTLE FASHION HOTEL
budacastlehotelbudapest.com
This smart hotel in the Castle District has 25 contemporary spacious rooms. There's no restaurant (beyond the breakfast room).
🚇 A7 ✉ I, Úri utca 39 ☎ 1 224 7900 🚊 16, 16A, 116

CARLTON HOTEL
carltonhotel.hu
A modern hotel on the Buda side of the river. Tucked down a quiet street at the foot of Fishermen's Bastion (▷ 25) and close to the Chain Bridge (▷ 4), it is convenient for sightseeing on both sides of the Danube.
🚇 B8 ✉ I, Apor Péter utca 3 ☎ 1 224 0999 🚇 Batthyany tér 🚊 Tram: 19, 41

CONTINENTAL HOTEL
continentalhotelbudapest.com
An elegant hotel with excellent facilities, including a rooftop swimming pool, saunas and a decent-sized fitness room. The Araz Restaurant is also a very good choice for your evening meal.
🚇 E8 ✉ VII, Dohány utca 42-44 ☎ 1 815 1061 🚇 Blaha Lujza tér 🚊 5, 7, 8E, 112, 178; trolley bus: 74

DANUBIUS HEALTH SPA RESORT MARGITSZIGET
danubiushotels.com
This large hotel on Margaret Island makes use of three local thermal springs and offers an extensive range of spa and beauty treatments.
🚇 D2 ✉ XIII, Margitsziget ☎ 1 889 4700 🚊 26, 106; tram: 1

HOTEL GELLÉRT
danubiushotels.com
One of the city's classic hotels, the art nouveau-style Gellért stands beside

Freedom Bridge and was first opened in 1918. Its rooms vary in size; those facing the river can be noisy because of the trams running below. Guests have one free access to the adjacent baths (▷ 41). The hotel is looking a little tired and is in need of some refurbishment—it's long been promised but keeps being deferred.

🔲 D10 ✉ XI, Szent Gellért tér 1 ☎ 1 889 5500 🚌 7, 133E; tram: 19, 47, 49

BREAKFAST

Breakfast is usually included in the price of a hotel stay—although a few of the upper-end hotels charge extra, so it's worth checking in advance. The fare is generally a buffet spread. The choice varies from place to place, but will always include salami, cheese, bread and cereals, and will often offer fruit, yoghurt and hot options like scrambled egg, bacon and sausages.

HOTEL PARLAMENT

parlament-hotel.hu

Located a short distance to the east of Parliament, this hotel has bold and modern rooms and the public areas are all strikingly designed. Guests can relax in the sauna and lounge bar and enjoy a buffet breakfast.

🔲 D6 ✉ V, Kálmán Imre utca 19 ☎ 1 374 6000 🚇 Kossuth tér 🚌 9, 15, 115; trolleybus: 70, 72, 73, 78

K+K HOTEL OPERA

kkhotels.com

Standing on a street near the State Opera House (▷ 52), the large K+K Hotel Opera has bright rooms and facilities that include a bar, bistro, sauna and gym.

🔲 D7 ✉ VI, Révay utca 24 ☎ 1 269 0222 🚇 Opera 🚌 105; trolley-bus: 70, 78

MÁTYÁS CITY HOTEL

cityhotel.hu

This imposing, neo-classical-style hotel stands beside Elizabeth Bridge in the heart of the Belváros. Its huge cellar restaurant has a medieval theme. The rooms are functional rather than elegant. Try to book one with a river view.

🔲 D9 ✉ V, Március 15 tér 7–8 ☎ 1 318 0595 🚇 Ferenciek tere 🚌 5, 7, 8E, 15; tram: 2

MERCURE BUDAPEST CITY CENTER

mercure.com

The large hotel is located in the middle of the action on Budapest's prime tourist street. Its rooms are contemporary in style and there's a lobby café for drinks and snacks.

🔲 D9 ✉ V, Váci utca 20 ☎ 1 485 3100 🚇 Vörösmarty tér/Ferenciek tere 🚌 5, 7, 15

RADISSON BLU BÉKE

radisson.com

First opened in 1914, the Béke preserves its original facade but has modern amenities including a swimming pool and fitness area. Its rooms are a good standard and the Zsolnay Café is a popular spot for a relaxing coffee and cake.

🔲 D6 ✉ VI, Teréz körút 43 ☎ 1 889 3900 🚇 Nyugati pályaudvar 🚌 91, 191, 291; trolley-bus: 72, 73; tram: 4, 6

ZARA BOUTIQUE HOTEL

boutiquehotelbudapest.com

In a superb position, the Zara draws on Oriental influences in its furnishings. Its compact rooms offer flat-screen TVs and internet access. Its Araz Bistro serves food and cocktails

🔲 D10 ✉ V, Só utca 6 ☎ 1 920 2100 🚌 15; tram: 2, 47, 49

Luxury Hotels

ARIA HOTEL

ariahotelbudapest.com

Found near the Basilica, this luxurious, music-themed hotel is one of the city's newcomers, and has quickly established itself among the very top rank. There's a rooftop bar, an underground spa, and 49 fabulously furnished rooms.

D8 V, Hercegprímás utca 5 1 445 4055 Bajcsy-Zsilinszky út or Deák tér 9, 105

CORINTHIA GRAND HOTEL ROYAL

corinthia.com

In a landmark building with a soaring glass atrium, the lovely Corinthia Grand on the Great Boulevard has immaculate rooms, an impressive marble lobby, a brasserie and oriental restaurant, and a stunning spa.

E7 VII, Erzsébet körút 43–49 1 479 4000 Blaha Lujza tér Trolley-bus: 70, 74, 78; tram: 4, 6

FOUR SEASONS HOTEL GRESHAM PALACE

fourseasons.com/budapest/

The Four Seasons, located at the end of the Chain Bridge, occupies the art-nou-veau edifice built for a British insurance company in the early 20th century. It's one of the country's most luxurious hotels with opulent rooms, an infinity pool in the top-floor, a health club and spa, a traditional coffeehouse and a relaxed restaurant.

C8 V, Széchenyi István tér 5–6 1 268 6000 Vörösmarty tér 15, 16, 105; tram: 2

HILTON BUDAPEST

danubiushotels.com

With a daring design that blends tinted glass with the remains of a medieval Dominican monastery, the Hilton stands on the main square in the Castle District and its river-facing rooms offer some of the best views in the city.

B7 I, Hess András tér 1–3 1 889 6600 16, 16A, 116

KEMPINSKI HOTEL CORVINUS

kempinski. com

Boldly modern, this large classy hotel in the Belváros has stylishly furnished rooms, several excellent restaurants, a luxury spa with gym and indoor pool and even its own art gallery showcasing young talent.

D8 V, Erzsébet tér 7–8 1 429 3777 Deák tér 15, 16, 105

MAMAISON ANDRÁSSY HOTEL

mamaison.com

This Bauhaus-style, luxury boutique hotel located among the villas and embassies toward the far end of Andrássy út has spacious rooms and the highly rated La Perle Noire restaurant (▷ 98).

F6 VI, Andrássy út 111 1 462 2100 Bajza utca 105

RITZ-CARLTON BUDAPEST

ritzcarlton.com

The latest five-star hotel in Budapest has 200 rooms, and a perfectly central location. While its furnishings evoke yesteryear Hungary with a distinctly modern edge, the atmosphere is relaxed and informal, and it has an informal grill restaurant. Some rooms have charming views.

D8 V, Erzsébet tér 1 429 5500 Deák tér 16, 105; tram: 47, 49

Here is key information to help smooth your path both before you go and when you arrive. It gives you all you need to know about local transport, useful websites and the best of the city's annual events.

Planning Ahead

When to Go

Budapest can get very hot in high season (May to September). Autumn is pleasantly mild and the hues of the Buda Hills are lovely, while the Spring Festival is the country's leading cultural event. In December, Christmas markets provide seasonal cheer.

TIME
Budapest is 1 hour ahead of London and 6 hours ahead of New York.

AVERAGE DAILY MAXIMUM TEMPERATURES

JAN	FEB	MAR	APR	MAY	JUN	JUL	AUG	SEP	OCT	NOV	DEC
57°F	59°F	63°F	67°F	71°F	77°F	81°F	82°F	79°F	72°F	63°F	58°F
14°C	15°C	17°C	20°C	21°C	25°C	27°C	28°C	26°C	22°C	17°C	15°C

Spring begins in late March and lasts until around mid-May. It is characterized by mild temperatures and regular showers.

Summer months are steamy, and it is not uncommon for temperatures in July and August to hit 35°C or higher. Many locals head for Lake Balaton to cool down.

Autumn starts fairly warm before becoming cooler and wetter, with occasional fog. It is an ideal time for cycling or walking in the hills to the west.

Winter temperatures dip sharply from mid-November. December and January are the coldest months. There is snow every year, but it does not last for long.

WHAT'S ON

March/April *Spring Festival:* The main festival of culture, with a fortnight of music and dance events held at numerous venues across the city.

May *Jazz Spring* at the Palace of Arts; *Festival of Museums* in the gardens of the National Museum.

June *Beer Festivals* in parks, streets and squares, and at Buda Castle.

June–August *Summer Festival* with open-air theater, musicals and children's events.

August *Sziget Festival:* Massive rock festival on Shipyard Island featuring international acts. *Festival of Folk Art:* Workshops and displays of craftwork in Buda Castle. *St. Stephen's Day:* Huge fireworks display by the Danube on 20 August.

August–September *Jewish Festival:* Celebration of Jewish heritage and culture, including concerts in the Great Synagogue.

September *International Wine Exhibition and Fair:* The main wine growers display their wares at Buda Castle; there's a procession and other events. *Cultural Heritage Days:* Normally closed buildings open up to view.

October *Café Budapest:* The autumn festival of contemporary art, dance and drama.

December *Christmas Market:* Vörösmarty tér and Liszt Ferenc tér are filled with stalls selling wooden and glass gifts throughout December. *New Year's Eve Gala Concert:* Feast and ball at the State Opera House.

Budapest Online
festivalcity.hu
This website lists up-to-date information about the city's festivals, including precise dates, acts and venues.

budapestinfo.hu
You can get an excellent introduction to the city on the website of the Budapest tourist office. As well as an overview of the city's history and sights, there is information about museums, transport, accommodation and more.

gotohungary.com
The website of the Hungarian National Tourist Office gives details of Budapest and the country as a whole and has a trip planner facility.

budapesttimes.hu
Online version of the city's leading English-language newspaper.

bkv.hu
bkk.hu
Useful websites covering the Budapest public-transport system. They include information on routes and ticket prices.

funzine.hu
The online companion to the free English-language listings magazine, with practical information, details of culture, restaurants, shops, family events and leisure activities.

caboodle.hu
An entertaining site with information on bars, restaurants, nightclubs and much more.

visitbudapest.travel
A site providing details of restaurants, nightlife and things to see and do.

welovebudapest.com
Provides events programs, news and fun articles about what's happening in Budapest.

TRAVEL SITES

theaa.com
A great resource for the essentials, ranging from destination information to travel insurance policies. There is also a UK facility for ordering travel guides and maps online.

fodors.com
A complete travel-planning site. You can research prices and weather; book air tickets, cars and rooms; ask questions (and get answers) from fellow visitors; and find links to other sites.

INTERNET ACCESS

Hotels of all ranges now offer free WiFi as standard, and many cafés also have codes providing complimentary WiFi access.

Getting There

ENTRY REQUIREMENTS

For the latest passport and visa information, check your relevant Hungarian embassy website before you travel.
UK: mfa.gov.hu
USA: washington.kormany.hu

FLIGHT TIMES

Flights from the UK to Budapest take about 2 hours 30 minutes. Direct journeys from New York take around 10 hours.

ARRIVING BY BOAT

A hydrofoil service run by Mahart Passnave (☎ 1 484 4013; mahartpassnave.hu) operates along the Danube, connecting Budapest with Bratislava and Vienna between June and late September. There are also services to towns on the Danube Bend.

AIRPORTS

Ferenc Liszt International Airport (BUD), formerly known as Ferihegy Airport, is 20km (12.5 miles) to the southeast of Budapest and is Hungary's main airport. It has two adjacent terminals, 2A and 2B.

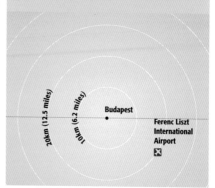

20km (12.5 miles)
10km (6.2 miles)
Budapest
Ferenc Liszt International Airport ✈

ARRIVING BY AIR

Budapest's Ferenc Liszt International Airport (tel 1 296 7000, bud.hu) is served by many of the major airlines. The most popular airlines flying from London's airports include British Airways from Heathrow, easyJet from Gatwick, Ryanair from Stansted and Wizz Air from Luton.

From New York John F Kennedy International Airport, Swiss flies to Budapest via Zurich, Austrian via Vienna, Delta Airlines via Paris, Lufthansa and United Airlines via Frankfurt and American Airlines via London on a codeshare with British Airways.

There are several ways of getting from the airport to the city hub, the least expensive being by public transport. Bus No. 200E stops outside terminal 2 and goes to Kőbánya-Kispest metro station (blue line 3), from where it is about 25 minutes to Deák tér. Bus and metro tickets cost 350Ft (single) at metro station, hotels and other outlets.

The closest railway station is Ferihegy, reached by bus No. 200E (night bus 900). Trains go to Nyugati station and it costs 465Ft for a single ticket.

If you'd like to be taken direct to your hotel or another address within the city limits, consider the Midibud Airport Shuttle (tel 1 550 0000); you book a ticket at the dedicated desk in the arrivals hall or online at midibud.hu, and it costs from 4,400Ft single or 7,900Ft return per person to the city centre (phone 24 hours before your departure to arrange the return pick-up point).

If there are several of you, it can be cheaper per person to take a taxi. The official airport taxi company—with desks at the airport—is called Főtaxi (tel 1 222 2222, fotaxi.hu). A ride to city hotels should cost around 6,500Ft, depending on traffic conditions. Never simply hail a taxi from outside the terminals. Your hotel should also be able to arrange a taxi when you depart Budapest.

ARRIVING BY BUS

In Hungary, the national company (operating under the Eurolines umbrella) is Volánbusz (tel 1 382 0888, volanbusz.hu), offering long-distance domestic and international services to countries including the UK, Austria, Germany, France and Spain. The UK operator is National Express (tel 08717 818181, nationalexpress.com). The main bus station in Budapest is Népliget International.

ARRIVING BY TRAIN

The three main railway stations in Budapest are the Eastern (Keleti), Western (Nyugati) and Southern (Déli), the first of which receives most international services. Each of the stations is linked to the metro system. The state railway company is called MÁV (tel 1 444 4499, elvira.hu for timetables and ticketing information). A journey from the UK by rail will take nearly 24 hours and is not cheap. It is more likely that passengers will be arriving from cities in neighboring countries, such as Kiev, Zagreb, Vienna, Bratislava, Belgrade or Bucharest. (Train travel however is a very viable option for onward journeys or even day trips out of the city.)

ARRIVING BY CAR

Hungary has five motorways (highways) radiating out from Budapest. The M1 connects the capital with Györ and Vienna, the M3 heads towards Ukraine, the M5 to Serbia, M6 and M7 to Croatia. Drivers using the Austria route cross into Hungary at Hegyeshalom and take the M1 motorway for two hours to Budapest. A toll applies on all motorways (highways) in Hungary; you can buy the prepaid toll pass (e-vignette) at many petrol (gas) stations or online at autopalyamatrica.hu. A 10-day e-vignette costs 2,975Ft. Remember that in Hungary the legal alcohol limit for driving is zero. Citizens of European Union countries may use their national driver's licences, while other citizens require an international licence. Drivers with insurance from countries that are members of licence-plate agreements with Hungary (including the UK) are covered for liability; citizens from other countries must present a green card (without one, they must take out insurance at the border before entering the country).

Getting Around

BUDGET CARD

BUDAPEST CARD

The Budapest Card—a discount card (valid for 24 hours at 4,500Ft, 48 hours at 7,500Ft or 72 hours at 8,900Ft) giving free access to many museums and reductions at selected restaurants and other sights—also allows free travel for one adult and child (under 14).

VALIDATING TICKETS

You should always validate your ticket at punching machines aboard trams, buses and trolley-buses or at the entrance to metro stations. Inspectors patrol the public transport system to check tickets. If you are caught without a valid ticket (a ticket that has not been punched), you can be fined 6,000Ft on the spot; however, tourists are usually offered the opportunity to purchase a three-day pass instead of the fine. Inspectors on the metro wear a blue uniform, while those on other modes of transport may be in plain clothes. Be sure to satisfy yourself that the inspectors are genuine before paying a fine; officials will carry formal identification.

METRO, BUSES, TRAMS AND TROLLEY-BUSES

● Budapest has four metro lines (including the first built in continental Europe), 34 tram lines, 15 trolley-bus routes and over 200 bus routes, as well as five suburban railway lines (called the HÉV). All fall under the control of Budapest Transport Ltd (known as BKV). Most public transport runs between the hours of 5am and 11pm, although there are also more than 30 night buses (all of which bear three digits starting with the number 9).

● Tickets are valid for use on all modes of public transport within the city limits (although not on the HÉV outside Budapest—you must buy extension tickets for journeys to stations beyond) and are available at metro stations, hotels, newsagents and tourist offices. These can be bought individually (350Ft) or in books of 10 (3,000Ft) tickets; a single ticket entitles you to one journey without changing trains. In addition, you can buy tourist transport tickets valid for one (1,650Ft), three (4,150Ft) or seven (4,400Ft) days granting unlimited travel within the city boundaries. Although you can purchase tickets from the driver on buses and trolley-buses, they are more expensive than prepaid ones and you will require the exact change (450Ft).

● The four metro lines are numbered and color-coded—Metro 1 (yellow) runs largely underneath Andrássy út (from Vörösmarty tér to Mexikói út); Metro 2 (red) is the only line to straddle the river, going west–east (Széll Kálmán tér to Őrs vezér tere); Metro 3 (blue) follows the river in an arc from north to south (Újpest-Központ to Kőbánya-Kispest); Metro 4 (green) goes from Keleti pu to Kelenföld vasútállomás.

● You'll find information on prices, tickets, timetables and routes at bkk.hu. Maps, discount cards and other information are available from Tourinform offices.

● See panel (left) for validating tickets—fines are easily incurred.

TAXIS

In the past, Budapest had a problem with high numbers of unscrupulous drivers overcharging tourists. However, in 2013 the system was overhauled to make this more difficult. All taxis now must be painted yellow and abide by a fixed scale of fares. Check that the meter is reset to the base rate (450Ft in daytime) and after that you will be charged 280Ft per kilometer. You should tip taxi drivers around 10 percent; fares can be paid by card. Some reliable taxi companies are: City Taxi: 1 211 1111; Főtaxi: 1 222 2222; Taxi 2000: 1 200 0000 and 6x6 Taxi: 1 266 6666.

CAR RENTAL

Budapest is easily navigable by public transport and on foot; driving can be awkward (with many one-way streets and limited parking). However, if you do wish to rent a car you will find all the major international companies are represented. You must be 21 or over, and show a driver's licence valid for a year or more and a passport. Some rental companies will deliver the car to your hotel.
● Avis can be found at Ferenc Liszt International Airport terminal 2B (tel 1 296 6421, avis.hu).
● Fox Autorent is at VII, Hársfa utca 53–55 (behind Corinthia Hotel, tel 1 382 9000, fox-autorent.com).

OTHER LOCAL TRANSPORT

Budapest also has a funicular railway (Sikló, ascending Castle Hill from Clark Ádám tér; tickets 1,200Ft one-way, 1,800Ft return), the Cogwheel Railway (running into the Buda Hills from Városmajor station, near Széll Kálmán tér, to Széchenyi-hegy; normal transport tickets are accepted), the Children's Railway (from Széchenyi-hegy to Hűvösvölgy stations; tickets 600Ft one-way, 1,200Ft return), and the Libegő, an atmospheric chairlift that connects Zugliget and János Hill in the Buda Hills (the journey is just over 1km, and takes 15 minutes; tickets 1,000Ft one-way, 1,400Ft return).

VISITORS WITH DISABILITIES

While facilities for those with limited mobility are improving in Budapest, it's true that many streets and public buildings remain difficult. Several buses now have low floors and ramps, including buses 5, 7, 9, 15, 16, 26 and 173. Trams 4 and 6 and trolley-bus 70 have low floors. Other routes have fewer regular buses and trolley-buses suitable for disabled passengers; these are indicated on timetables with a wheelchair symbol. For information, contact National Federation of Disabled Persons (MEOSZ; meoszinfo.hu).

TOURIST OFFICES

Tourinform offices (tourinform.hu):
✉ Terminal 2B ☎ 1 438 8080 🕐 Daily 8–10 (24 Dec 8–2; 25 Dec, 1 Jan 10–6)
✉ V, Sütő utca 2 (Deák tér) ☎ 1 438 8080 🕐 Daily 8–8 (24 Dec 8–1; 25, 26 Dec, 1 Jan 10–6)

Essential Facts

EMERGENCY NUMBERS

- Ambulance ☎ 104
- Fire service ☎ 105
- Police ☎ 107
- International emergency hotline ☎ 112
- British embassy
  ✉ VI, Harmincad utca 6
  ☎ 1 266 2888; gov.uk
- US embassy
  ✉ V, Szabadság tér 12
  ☎ 1 475 4400;
  hungary.usembassy.gov
- Irish embassy
  ✉ V, Bank Centre,
  Szabadság tér 7 ☎ 1 301 4960; embassyofireland.hu

MONEY

The Hungarian currency is the forint (abbreviated to HUF or Ft). It is circulated as coins up to 100Ft and as notes above that up to 20,000Ft.

SMOKING BAN

Smoking is banned inside public spaces (including pubs, clubs, cafés and restuarants).

CITY LAYOUT

Budapest is bisected by the Danube, which runs from north to south. Buda lies on the western side and Pest on the eastern side, and they are connected by a total of 12 bridges (six of them in the centre). Beyond that, the city is divided into 23 districts; the two middle digits of a postcode indicates the district in which an address falls—so, for example, an address with the postcode H-1051 would be in District V.

ELECTRICITY

● Current in Hungary is 230 volts AC (50Hz). Plug adaptors are needed to match the standard European two-prong sockets. A transformer is needed for appliances operating on 110–120 volts.

MAIL

The main post office in Budapest can be found at:
● Nyugati Railway Station, at VI, Teréz körút 51, open Mon–Fri 7am–8pm, Sat 8–6. Smaller post offices are usually open on weekdays between 8am and 6pm. There are sometimes post offices inside large shopping malls. Within Hungary, letters up to 30g cost 120Ft to send and those up to 100g cost 235Ft. A standard letter up to 50g will cost 495Ft to send to Europe and 640Ft to elsewhere in the world; postcards are 240Ft to Europe and 280Ft beyond. You can cash travellers' cheques in post offices, wire money abroad, and settle fines for parking and speeding offences.

OPENING HOURS

● Shops: Mon–Fri 9–6, Sat 9–1. Some food stores and most shopping malls will open longer hours, the latter often including Sundays.
● Banks: Mon–Fri 8–4. Some banks will also open on Saturday, although all are closed on Sunday. Many ATMs are within the bank entrance; you can usually access these out of hours by swiping your bank card through the electronic reader outside.

● Restaurants: Usually open daily 11–11, although it's not unusual for some to close on Sunday and for others to close for a few hours between lunch and dinner.

PUBLIC HOLIDAYS

Attractions, shops, bars and restaurants may be closed on the following dates:
● 1 January
● 15 March (commemorating the 1848 revolution)
● Easter Monday
● Good Friday
● 1 May (Labour Day)
● Whit Monday (Pentecost)
● 20 August (St. Stephen's Day)
● 23 October (commemorating the 1956 revolution)
● 1 November (All Saints' Day)
● 25 and 26 December (Christmas)

TELEPHONES

● The country code for Hungary is 0036, and the city code is 1.
● Budapest phone numbers (excluding the main city code) are seven digits in length.
● For domestic calls from Budapest to areas beyond the city, dial 06, followed by the relevant area code and then the specific telephone number.
● Calls to mobiles from a landline require the 06 prefix followed by the code of the relevant mobile phone provider and then the specific telephone number.
● The majority of public telephones accept coins, as well as phone cards, which can be purchased at newsagents and post offices.
● The number for domestic directory enquiries is 198 and international 199.
● To call the UK from Hungary, dial 0044, followed by the area code (minus its first zero) and the number required.
● To call the US from Hungary, the international code is 001. To dial Hungary, the international code is 0036.

PRECAUTIONS

Budapest is generally a safe city, although visitors should avoid walking alone in some areas beyond the heart of the city after dark. Pickpocketing is common at railway stations and other places frequented by tourists. There are also regular reports of men being conned into buying women drinks in certain bars and then being presented with enormous bills (and being forced to pay by burly staff). Always check taxi meters are re-set and study restaurant bills carefully to avoid being overcharged.

Language

Hungarian (Magyar) belongs to the Finno-Ugric group of languages, rather than Indo-European like most of Europe's languages. Consequently understanding and speaking Hungarian poses great difficulty to foreigners even though its spelling is logical. English and German are widely spoken in Budapest and hotel staff may speak several languages. However, learning a few words of the local language will be met with appreciation.

THE BASICS

yes/no	*igen/nem*
please	*kérek*
thank you	*köszönöm*
excuse me	*elnézést*
hello	*szia*
good morning	*jó reggelt*
good afternoon	*jó napot*
good evening	*jó estét*
goodbye	*viszontlátásra*
do you speak English?	*beszél angolul?*
I don't understand	*nem értem*

AT THE HOTEL

single room	*egyágyas szoba*
double room	*dupla szoba*
with/without bathroom	*fürdőszobá(val)/ nélkül*
breakfast	*reggeli*
lunch	*ebéd*
dinner	*vacsora*
how much?	*mennyibe kerül?*
do you accept credit cards?	*elfogad hitelkár- tyát?*

FINDING HELP

I need a doctor/ dentist	*orvost/fogorvost keresek*
can you help me?	*tud segíteni?*
where is the hospital?	*hol van a kórház?*
where is the police station?	*hol van a rendőrség?*

NUMBERS

1	*egy*
2	*kettő*
3	*három*
4	*négy*
5	*öt*
6	*hat*
7	*hét*
8	*nyolc*
9	*kilenc*
10	*tíz*
11	*tizenegy*
12	*tizenkettő*
13	*tizenhárom*
14	*tizennégy*
15	*tizenöt*
16	*tizenhat*
17	*tizenhét*
18	*tizennyolc*
19	*tizenkilenc*
20	*húsz*
21	*huszonegy*
30	*harminc*
40	*negyven*
50	*ötven*
60	*hatvan*
70	*hetven*
80	*nyolcvan*
90	*kilencven*
100	*száz*
1,000	*ezer*

AT THE RESTAURANT

restaurant	*étterem*
menu	*étlap*
beer	*sör*
wine	*bor*
white/red	*fehér/vörös*
cheers	*egészségedre*
water	*víz*
bread	*kenyér*
orange juice	*narancslé*
the bill please	*kérem a számlát*

GETTING AROUND

airport	*repülőtér*
ticket	*jegy*
one-way	*egy útra*
round-trip	*retúr*
bus stop	*buszmegálló*
train	*vonat*
station	*állomás*
tram	*villamos*
boat	*hajó*
entry fee	*belépő*
free	*ingyenes*
child	*gyermek*
adult	*felnőtt*
where is/are...?	*hol van...?*
here/there	*itt/ott*
turn left/right	*balra/jobbra forduljon*
straight on	*egyenesen*
when/what time?	*mikor?*
today	*ma*
yesterday	*tegnap*
tomorrow	*holnap*
how long?	*mennyi idő?*

SHOPPING

market	*piac*
what time do you open/close?	*mikor nyit/zár?*
do you have?	*van...?*

Timeline

THE EARLY YEARS

People have lived on the site that is now Budapest for several thousand years. The Romans extended the eastern border of their empire to the Danube after they arrived in the 1st century BC. They remained for four centuries, and Aquincum became capital of Pannonia Inferior.

PEASANT REVOLT

The Peasant Revolt was led by György Dózsa, a man who had received acclaim for his bravery during struggles against the Ottomans. The uprising was crushed, and Dózsa suffered a painful death being roasted on a metal throne and devoured by some of his fellow rebels, who had been starved by their captors.

Orthodox Synagogue; sphinx at the Opera House; equestrian statues on Heroes' Square; roof of the Elephant House at the Zoo; detail of a fountain; the Calvinist Church (left to right)

1st century BC The Romans (▷ panel, left) arrive at what is now Budapest toward the end of the century.

AD 896 The Magyar tribes settle in the area.

1000 King Stephen is crowned as the first king of Hungary, and establishes the country as a Christian state.

1241–42 The Mongols invade and devastate the country. King Béla IV fortifies Castle Hill against future attacks.

1458–90 The reign of King Matthias, during which Buda becomes one of the capitals of Renaissance Europe.

1514 The Peasant Revolt (▷ panel, left).

1541 The Turks invade and occupy Buda. They remain for 150 years.

1686 Buda is liberated by an allied European army. Hungary comes under the control of the Habsburgs.

1825 The Age of Reform begins, during which public institutions like the National Theater and the National Museum are established.

1848–49 War of Independence. Revolution breaks out on 15 March, during which poet Sándor Petőfi addresses a crowd

outside the National Museum. The Habsburgs eventually prove victorious.

1867 The Compromise is agreed, establishing a dual monarchy between Austria and Hungary.

1873 Pest, Buda and Óbuda are officially unified to form the single city of Budapest.

1896 The Millennial Celebrations, commemorating the anniversary of the Magyar conquest.

1944–45 After entering secret negotiations with the Allies, Hungary is occupied by the Germans. Budapest is "liberated" by the Russians after a savage siege of Castle Hill.

1956 Revolution breaks out on 23 October, but is suppressed by a vast army of Soviet tanks. Hundreds of thousands flee the country.

1989 The fall of communism. Free elections are announced.

2004 Hungary joins the European Union.

2015 Hungary takes over the presidency of the International Holocaust Remembrance Alliance (IHRA).

2016 Budapest Zoo's 150th anniversary.

2018 Parliamentary elections due. Viktor Orbán will aim to win for a fourth time.

THE GREAT FLOOD

In 1838, a flood destroyed much of Pest—several monuments bear markers showing the height reached by the waters. In the aftermath, city planners were able to start again and today's layout dates to that period.

TREATY OF TRIANON

Hungary was penalized heavily after its defeat during World War I. The Treaty of Trianon in 1920 stripped it of two-thirds of its territory, something that remains a sore point for Hungarians to this day.

NEED TO KNOW TIMELINE

Index

Titles in the Series

- Amsterdam
- Bangkok
- Barcelona
- Boston
- Brussels and Bruges
- Budapest
- Chicago
- Dubai
- Dublin
- Edinburgh
- Florence
- Hong Kong
- Istanbul
- Krakow
- Las Vegas
- Lisbon
- London
- Madrid
- Melbourne
- Milan
- Montréal
- Munich
- New York City
- Orlando
- Paris
- Rome
- San Francisco
- Seattle
- Shanghai
- Singapore
- Sydney
- Tokyo
- Toronto
- Venice
- Vienna
- Washington, D.C.